WHAT IF YOU DON'T BREAK DOWN

Contact Tony at 1894tony@gmail.com

This book is dedicated to my wife Patricia, who is as happy to let me go off on my bike as she is to have me back.

For that and so much more I am eternally grateful.

CONTENTS

1 - INTRODUCTION

It seems like a lifetime ago that I passed my motorcycle test, and in truth given that it was a little over 40 years ago then in some respects it is a lifetime.

I was 17 when I passed my test and I've done a few miles on bikes since then. In fact, I reckon I've done around 45,000 of those miles on European trips travelling fairly extensively across much of Western Europe.

This book is about one of those trips and it's a trip of two parts.

The first part of the trip is with three friends as travelling companions as we head from the Spanish Port of Bilbao, into the Pyrenees and onto the Cote d'Azur in France.

The second part of the trip is an adventure on my own that took me down the Mediterranean coast of Italy to fulfil a long standing dream to ride the Amalfi coast road, before crossing to the Adriatic coast, then back inland through Tuscany and Umbria and across the Gulf of Venice through Slovenia and the Dolomites before heading for Rotterdam and home via northern Italy, Austria, Germany, Luxembourg and Belgium.

Many of the words in this book were written on the road, and in that sense the words tell their own story as the trip unfolded.

I suppose there are few people that travel and change the world but there are probably few people that have travelled and haven't been changed by the world they have seen and experienced.

2 - WHAT IF YOU DON'T BREAK DOWN?

Over the years I've stopped and chatted with many bikers, some of whom have gone out and made their travel dreams happen but I've met plenty more who for one reason or another haven't.

To be honest there are few of my bike trips these days where at some point I don't recall the words of a biker I met a few years ago.

As we chatted over coffee and talked about motorcycle travel in Europe he told me he was put off by worrying about what would happen if he broke down.

And while it makes nothing but good sense to have to have some sort of back up in place, whether that's a roll of repair tape, some cable ties or travel insurance, you most definitely don't need to spend time wondering and worrying about what will happen if you break down – better to spend time thinking of what might happen if you don't.

I don't think there's anything particularly hardy or brave about travelling on your own on a motorbike and I don't suppose I'm convinced that you need to be a particular type of person to enjoy it nor do I think you need to spend endless hours poring over the smallest details.

I've had fantastic times, seen some great sights and travelled on some amazing roads,
I've been hot and uncomfortable, wet and uncomfortable and cold and uncomfortable but for the most part I've been exhilarated and uplifted and the good bits far outweigh the bad bits many many times over.

I don't think you need to travel all the way around the world to have an adventure and I don't think you need to do something that you think other people will view as amazing.

In fact, I just think if it's something you want to do and you can make it happen then you should do it.

Whatever it was you were worried about will vanish once you start riding.

If something unplanned happens, you really will figure out a solution – there is a peacefulness about travelling on your own and a resourcefulness inside all of us that can solve almost anything, you just don't always find it until you have to.

At the same time as you're alone in a place that is strange to you, you'll probably find the overall experience and the general sense of adventure will leave you feeling more connected to the world than you have ever been.

Alternatively, you could spend an age worrying about the details, asking what other people think and wondering about what might happen if you break down, but what if it doesn't go wrong and what if it all goes right … and what if you do decide to make that trip and what if you **don't** break down?

3 - I'VE BEEN RIDING BIKES A LONG TIME

I haven't really got a precise record of how many miles I've done over the years.

I've never really kept a detailed account of them, there again I don't have a record of how many hot dinners I've had since I was born either, but I do know that I've done more miles than I've had hot dinners.

Even at my age if I'd had a hot dinner every day of my life then that's still less than 21,000 ... and I've definitely not had a hot dinner every day.

I've had a few bikes over the years since I passed my bike test, they've included, Honda's Suzuki's Moto Guzzi's and most recently my first Kawasaki – I even briefly had a scooter!

Aside from the usual holiday travel in Europe and beyond I've done a reasonable amount of European travel on my bikes and in cars and as I have already said whilst I don't have a precise record, I can make a reasonable estimate of the mileage.

It's probably somewhere around the 45,000-mile mark on bikes and maybe around the same in cars.

For those who have an interest in knowing what bikes I've done European trips on, they have been: Suzuki GSX-R's 600 (x2); GSX-R750; GSX-R 1,000; Honda Fireblade; Honda CB1000R and a Kawasaki Z1000SX.

Aside from the home countries of England, Scotland and Wales, my biking experiences include riding in Andorra, Austria, Belgium, Czech Republic, France, Germany, Holland, Italy, Lichtenstein, Luxembourg, Portugal, Slovenia, Spain and Switzerland.

My first biking trip across the channel was back in 2003 when two of us crossed from Portsmouth to Le Havre and then biked down to Le Mans in the Pays de la Loire region of France to watch the Moto GP racing.

Things didn't go quite as planned on that first trip – mainly down to the double booking of the hotel we were set to stay in for a few days – the result of which meant that we ended up heading to the circuit and sleeping in the Grandstand on the start/finish straight.

I've travelled on good roads and bad roads. Some of them have scared me a little, some have bored me a little and others have drawn me back on more than one occasion.

Accommodation has often been great, occasionally poor, sometimes in the middle of towns and cities and sometimes in the middle of nowhere and on one occasion high up a mountain.

I've taken my bikes on the short ferry crossings from Dover to Calais, the North Sea crossings via Hull to Rotterdam and Zeebrugge, the channel crossing from Portsmouth to Le Havre and also the long trips down to Bilbao and Santander in Spain from the ferry terminals in Portsmouth and Plymouth on the south coast. In addition to taking the boat I've done the Eurotunnel crossing via Folkestone/Calais a few times.

I've also *'been down the road'* when traveling in Europe as well – back in 2012 I was hit from behind whilst approaching a toll booth on the A55 Italian Autostrada that bypasses the major north Italian city of Turin – it wasn't a great experience and left my Honda CB1000R and my body damaged.

I've learned a few things on my trips – perhaps the most basic being an early lesson that using a rucksack for luggage isn't always the most comfortable way to travel!

Since that first trip I've organised another dozen or so with friends, with the group size normally ranging from four to six.

I've also made a couple of solo trips – the first in 2010 and the most recent in September 2015.

So I suppose all in all it's probably fair to say that one way or another, whether by accident or design, experience has taught me a thing or two.

I have learned that motorcycle travel in Europe can be pretty easy, that you can travel pretty cheaply if you want to and there is so much to see that you're more likely to grow old before you grow tired of the experiences that await you.

Really you just need to do it.

4 - BIKES AND KIT

Over the years I've done my European bike trips on a variety of different machines, and only one of those would be described as an obvious 'touring bike'.

My first trip was done on a 2003 Suzuki GSX-R 600. It was a superb machine and finished in classic blue and white Suzuki colours, for those who recall the model it was the one with the white wheels and it sort of looked fast when it was standing still.

My luggage arrangements for that first trip consisted of me carrying all my gear in a rucksack on my back – which worked well to a point, apart from the points of things normally digging into my back.

Having all your gear on your back all day long can become pretty uncomfortable especially when you have bulky or harder items such as shoes, camera and phone chargers working their way around the pack and seemingly conspiring to dig into you at every opportunity.

Of course, you can aim to pack with the softer stuff against your back, but for me using a back pack for all your gear just isn't the way to do it.

Although I did use a rucksack on a number of subsequent trips I tended to make sure that it was only really waterproofs and the like that were carried on my back and I have often used the Kriega brand of travel luggage.

Despite their fairly unusual name Kriega are a British company based in Chester in the north west of England. They've been around for the last 15 or so years and they really do make some fabulous gear.

On subsequent trips, after my 2003 trip to Le Mans I pretty much tended to use the Kriega tail packs that simply strap down onto the rear seat of the bike, along with a combination of backpack and tank bag.

Various combinations of their luggage have been well tried and tested over the years by my traveling companions.

I first used the tail packs on my second trip, on another Suzuki GSX-R 600, this time it was a 2005 model.

Anyone setting their bike up for a trip away has an increasingly diverse range of luggage options to choose from and no doubt some of the decision making will come down to the type of bike being used and what luggage system works best with a particular model.

From a personal experience point of view, my Kriega gear has always served me well, remained 100% waterproof and I suppose it a testament to the company's confidence in their products that they offer a 10 year guarantee.

I've also toured on two other Suzuki's a 2007 GSX-R 750 and a 2008 GSX-R 1000 and like the two 600's I found them to be superb all day bikes.

I did a couple of European trips on the GSX-R 1000 and on one of those trips I did a shade under 4,000 miles in a fortnight, and I guess that some of the comfort factor is down to physique – at 5'7" I never really felt cramped on them, but I've seen plenty of taller guys getting off them and looking like they need time with a good physio to get their aching limbs sorted out.

It was only after an accident in 2010 that I developed chronic problems with my wrists and which pretty much made the head down/arse up stance of a sports bike, coupled with the increased pressure on my wrists too much of an uncomfortable proposition for me for anything other than the shortest of journeys.

The last 'full on' sports bike that I toured on was a 2009 Honda Fireblade CB1000 RR, this was another wonderful bike to rack off big miles on.

After that it was a 2011 Honda CB1000R which was another fine bike for touring – although with it being a 'naked' bike it did mean that any motorway miles were done with quite a wind blast which in itself could get uncomfortable.

Having said that, the windblast issue was never really too much of a problem as motorway miles have always been kept to a minimum and it was only ever really the drag down to the south coast from my home in the north west of England for the ferry or tunnel when I did extended motorway miles.

So I think my experience leads me to say that actually you can tour on most any bike – many will mean a compromise of one sort or another but I suspect there are few that you could say are downright unsuitable.

In any case, whatever compromises are made when touring by bike for several thousand miles, they are sure to be outweighed by the sheer experience of the travel and the ride.

New bike for the trip

In the spring of 2014 I traded my Honda CB1000R.

My decision to change bikes was very much with my 2015 trip in mind. I'd been quite taken by the press reports and reviews that I'd read about Kawasaki's new Z1000 SX.

The bike manages to combine superb performance with handling that's not a world away from a sports bike, along with an upright riding position and the ability to easily carry its integrated luggage in two decently sized panniers.

All in all it's a cracking all-rounder and worthy of its inclusion in the versatile sports tourer category of motorcycle – easy to ride, comfortable and more than capable of getting a shift on if you want it to. It was an easy decision to buy one of these after a decent test ride in the May of 2014.

There are probably as many opinions about sorting out a road trip and what to take as there are riders and it's not for me to say how you should organise it or what you should take, so my thoughts are just that - my own thoughts based on my experience and what works for me.

Some bikers think that using a Sat Nav on a bike is some form of heresy and in some ways, is the very antithesis of motorcycle touring, but for me it's just something to use alongside a map.

I tend to think along the lines of why waste time in towns and cities that you don't want to be in, or why waste time scouting around for petrol when a couple of quick taps on the gadget can save you all that bother.

And I've never bought into the school of thinking that to travel without a Sat Nav makes you any more of a purist biker than those who travel with one but I have come across bikers who will vehemently argue the opposite.

I do think having access to decent maps just makes good sense, there is so much you can do online now with Google Maps and Google Earth but for me there is little to beat the singular satisfaction of writing on a map or spreading a map out to plot an outline route and I love to look back at the end of the day or the end of a trip and be able to see where I've been.

Not only does it allow me to get a real sense of the journey I've made it also gives me a real sense of the journeys and travel I've yet to make.

When it comes to tools and spare parts for the bike I'm very firmly in the rather minimalist, less is more type of camp, maybe it's different if you're in some far flung place remote from civilisation but as my travels have been in western Europe I've always been reasonably confident that I'd be able to sort something out ... even if did mean falling back on my mobile 'phone and credit card!

That's not to say I travel without anything, but my tool kit is pretty much made up of: a couple of suitably sized allen keys (hex keys as some folk call them), a pair of pliers, a knife, some cable ties and some duct tape. My logic is fairly simple in so much as if a roadside repair needs much more than that then to be honest it's probably beyond my ability to fix it.

I never really take much cash and normally just start off with what's been left over from the last trip or holiday. I tend to get cash as and when I need it although I would caution against travelling with too little in some parts of Europe as it's not altogether unusual to come across places that will only take payment in cash.

When it comes to planning and whether or not to book accommodation in advance I think it's as simple as doing what works for you and what you're most comfortable with.

There are pros and cons to both and as with the Sat Nav question some folk have pretty strong views in favour of the no planning option.

When I've organised trips with friends I've pretty much planned and booked our accommodation in advance.

Our groups have typically tended to be sized between four and six - and getting rooms and secure parking for bikes is very easy to do online and in advance and there are plenty of options to book places that allow for cancellation at no cost with just 24 hours' notice, which can be ideal if circumstances change.

Some folk prefer the security and ease of travelling with one of the many companies that specialise in organised bike tours – that's not something I've ever fancied but if it's what works best for you then why not?

Whilst that form of travel isn't for me I can see why some folk are attracted to it and in any case, it beats sitting at home thinking of all the things that could go wrong.

Just about the only golden rule I would put forward is to say don't ever over pack – and whilst you might think that's not an option on a bike, it most definitely is.

I've seen people travelling on weekend trips with what looks like enough luggage for a couple of months away from home.

That's not to say that I would claim to have fully mastered the art of travelling light but I've most definitely learned from experience.

T shirts can be bought cheaply on your travels, socks and underwear can easily be washed through at night, or thrown away and if you are a bit lax with the washing a liberal amount of deodorant can be a godsend!

THE TRIP

In September 2015, I set off on my annual European road trip with friends. On this trip, there were four of us but it was to be a trip of two halves.

Part One would see four of us: Rich, Colin, Dave and I arrive in Bilbao and head across northern Spain, the Pyrenees and onto Digne Les Bains in France.

Part Two would see us go our own separate ways with Colin and Dave heading home via Baveno in the Italian Lakes, then on towards Germany and Luxembourg via the Gothard Pass in Switzerland – a great Pass that myself and friends have done a good few times over the years.

Rich had loose plans to head across to northern Italy, Austria and maybe Slovenia with nothing more specific than to do as many mountain passes as he could.

My own plan was to spend the next couple of weeks working my way down into Southern Italy, broadly down the Mediterranean side and then to come back up, broadly via the Adriatic Side, then maybe heading for Slovenia before turning for northern Italy, Germany, Luxembourg and home.

I had no particular fixed plan in mind other than I did want to do the Sorrento/Amalfi road and also the Stelvio Pass other than that I was open to whatever panned out and whatever the road ahead offered me.

I left my home in Manchester on the Tuesday morning to travel down to Wrecclesham, a small village with a population of around 3,000 or so on the outskirts of Farnham which is a much bigger town in Surrey with a population of around 40,000 and located some 28 miles from London.

My brother Mike and his wife Alison live there and in addition to always making me welcome, their place was an ideal stop over for the onward journey to Portsmouth as it's only around 35 miles or so from their home.

The journey to Wrecclesham from where I live in Manchester is about 240 miles and always seems like something of a chore, but as I said, my brothers place is a decent stop over with its proximity to Portsmouth and the other south coast ferry ports.

Portsmouth was where we were set to take the Brittany Ferries service to Bilbao. So for me the overnight stay at Mike and Alison's was just an ideal place to stay en route.

I suppose I could have taken a more scenic route rather than dragging out the majority of the trip on the motorways from Manchester.

The prospect of plenty of good roads to ride in the coming weeks made the journey tolerable. In practice, it was a largely uneventful journey. Boring yes but in practice uneventful.

One slight bonus that I managed to afford myself was to avoid the mind numbing experience of the M25 by taking a route that took me via Marlow in Buckinghamshire, which is about 35 miles west of central London.

For readers unfamiliar with the M25 it's a 117- mile stretch of motorway that pretty much circles Greater London and has the dubious honour of being the second longest city bypass in Europe and was built over a number of years with the final 13-mile stretch being opened in 1986.

Perhaps the best and most significant benefit of me travelling via Marlow, was that I was able to find a roadside snack bar where I had a decent sausage sandwich and coffee for what I thought was the quite reasonable price of £3.50

I arrived at my brothers around 15:45 and my friend Rich' who hadn't been able to leave at the time I did, due to work commitments, joined us around 20:30 that evening.

I don't really like people

Rich' is a fella I've known for maybe the last dozen years or so and he's a very experienced biker and more than competent on or off road as well as on track.

We've biked together locally, around our usual haunts of North Wales and Shropshire as well as a good number of short breaks in Wales and Scotland.

Rich' has been on quite a few of the European road trips and I think this one was probably about trip number eight for him, apart from that he's biked in Europe with other friends and on his own.

He's always got more than one bike in his garage, and in addition to his bike for this trip he has a Suzuki GSX-R 750 as well as an off road bike for a bit of green laning.

When he's not doing that he's either playing squash, doing a bit of rock climbing, hang gliding or the like and when he's not doing any of those then he's basically asleep for which he has a fine reputation!

His ride for this trip was a very attractive, almost to the point of pretty, Ducati Monster a bike that brought with it its own unique Italian mechanical soundtrack.

Rich is one of the few riders I know who can more than wring the neck out of any bike he sits on and this one was no exception.

Like the others I suppose you could describe him as a bit of a character and one on his own – after all how many people do you know that in their own words have said "I've come to the conclusion that I don't like people"

Mike and Ali provided the food, alcohol, bed and Wi-Fi as well as secure parking for the bikes. So at a stroke our needs were met – old Abraham Maslow would have been pleased, although I suppose the self-actualization at the top of his pyramid would have to wait for the roads of Spain at the earliest.

Mike was up and away early to work and after Alison left for her work Rich and I had breakfast, packed our gear up and were on our way for around 09:20.

Meet up

We didn't go directly to Portsmouth but headed for the roadside services outside the market town of Petersfield in East Hampshire where we were scheduled to meet with Colin (Col) and Dave who were traveling up from Sittingbourne in Kent.

Petersfield was probably less than a 20-mile ride for us and a little less than a 100 miles for Col and Dave and by 09:50 we'd met up, had a quick chat, toped up with petrol and we were on our way for the short journey to the Brittany ferry terminal in Portsmouth.

Col's another fella that I've biked with plenty of times and if it wasn't for the fact that he lives down in Kent I reckon we'd have biked many more miles together.

He made his first trip with our small group back in 2008 after he'd contacted me via an online forum with a general question about making a European trip.

Following that first online contact we spoke on the 'phone and have been firm friends ever since.

He's a good bloke, very funny and very generous and there have been quite a few occasions when he and his wife have literally made their home an open house for us all when we've been taking the Eurotunnel from Dover.

He's stayed with us in Manchester a number of times and I think has done about six European trips with us, as well as one of our Welsh weekend trips.

Col's another experienced biker. When we first met he had a Suzuki GSX-R 600 but has since had his share of Italian exotica with a couple of MV Agusta Brutale's – his current MV is a stunning Brutale Italia, and always presented in near concours condition.

Despite being the very proud owner of an MV Agusta his bike for this trip was a nine-year-old 600cc Honda Hornet, and I think it may have been the second or third European trip he's done on this machine ... basically as beautiful as his Brutale is, it gives him too much of a sore backside to put in a couple of thousand miles in ten days or so.

Although christened Colin by his parents he's actually better known to us as Shandy – namely because that's his preferred tipple.

The fourth and final traveling companion for Part One of this year's trip was Dave, Shandy's father.

Dave is a great bloke who we met for the first time somewhere in France a few years ago, when we were towards the back end of a road trip and heading towards home.

He and his wife Lynne (Shandy's mum) were also on a motorcycling holiday and we met up en route and shared some time and coffee with them. Since then we've caught up with them a few times when we've been down in Kent which is where they live.

Dave was scheduled to come on the 2014 trip with us when we biked down in the Black Forrest in south west Germany, but unfortunately had to pull out just a few weeks before we left due to family health reasons.

I couldn't even get close to saying how many bikes Dave has had, or even how many he currently has – in a word it's a lot.

I think the last time we were at his place he had about seven or eight and he has had (and has) his fair share of classics both British and Italian and has done a lot of biking in Europe, mainly in France.

He's an ace restorer as well, and there is little if anything, that any of us could teach him when it comes to bikes. His bike for this trip was a Suzuki Bandit that he'd bought just for the Road Trip.

The only person missing from this trip was a friend called Mick who had planned to travel with us but simply couldn't make this one due to health problems.

Rich, Shandy, Mick and I have biked together a lot and I don't think it can always be easy to fit in and get along quickly with a group that have been around together for a while – but maybe it says everything about Dave that he has always fitted in with us and this trip was to be no exception.

All aboard

Check in at Portsmouth was routine and we were straight onto the boat, the Brittany Ferries Cap Finistere for the 24-hour journey to Bilbao – we'd opted for the direct route rather than the longer 33 hours on the sailing that goes via Roscoff.

It was the first time I'd done this route and it's fair to say it was pretty decent. Check in and boarding were quick and easy and the Cap Finistere seemed like it would provide a pretty comfortable haven for our journey south.

The ship itself was built in 2001 but didn't join the Brittany Ferries fleet until 2010 and was big enough to carry more than 800 passengers and around 500 cars.

I gather the ship was named after the rock bound peninsula – Cape Finistere on the west coast of Spain.

In stark contrast to my experience with other ferry operators there were plenty of helpful crew members on hand to strap the bikes down almost the minute we got off them and to offer helpful advice and direction.

Going back a few years another major operator on the cross-channel ferry route used to do that, but in recent times have left the task of securing bikes to yourself at the same time as being explicitly clear about not taking any responsibility – it's a shame and I think a pretty disappointing stance to take.

The Brittany Ferries experience was good.

We had a bright and spacious cabin and a decent sized shower.

I'm not big or overweight but the showers in some of the cabins on other ferries really can be small and I reckon anyone who is only modestly overweight (or big) will have as much contact with the shower walls as they will with the water.

Without exception, the staff were pleasant and polite and it seemed to me that whatever they do in terms of customer handling training works.

The food on offer was as plentiful as it was good value and seemingly with enough variety to probably suit most palates.

The only thing that I would say is that the pictures and videos of the swimming pool that are offered on the Brittany Ferries web site are somewhat flattering in respect of the actual size ... but as we weren't making use of that facility I can't say I was bothered one way or the other.

There was also a range of other activities that included makeover and massage sessions, games room, kennels for dogs and various bars and food outlet's – the food and drink was enough for us and maybe not surprisingly we gave the makeover and massage sessions a miss.

I slept well, and as usual was up early. Unlike watching the sun rise over Manchester in the north west of England I was able to enjoy watching the most magnificent and glorious sunrise as we approached our destination in Spain.

Breakfast was good and great value at less than £8.00, and it wasn't long after taking breakfast that the boat was making its way into the industrial port of Bilbao some 10 miles south of the Bay of Biscay.

In fact, I think we had docked a little ahead of schedule but it was also probably the longest I've ever waited to get off a ferry, partly I suppose as we were down in what seemed like the bowels of the boat.

We'd agreed in advance that Rich and I would share the route planning for the first four days (after that we were set to head our separate ways).

It was my turn first and I'd planned a route to take us out of Bilbao, which is one of the most heavily populated areas of northern Spain with around a million or so people living there.

After that it was on to our first overnight stop at the Hotel Ekai located on the edge of the Pyrenees Mountains a mile or so from Aoiz and about 18 miles from Pamplona in the Navarra region of northern Spain.

The delay getting off the boat meant we were probably not on the road until getting on for 14.00 or so.

Our route took us to Durango, Ibarra, Zubieta and a few places in between and for much of our journey we had the Urkiola mountain range and its natural park to the south with its rugged limestone peaks providing a tremendous backdrop for our ride.

I have to say that the last hour or so of riding probably matched or came close to anything that I'd done previously – not so much in terms of scenery, although of course the Pyrenees is hardly unattractive, but more so in terms of non-stop bend after bend after bend on very decent well surfaced roads that were all but empty.

It really was constant for the last hour or so and for the most part we sped along around the 80 to 100mph mark.

The hotel had great reviews on the booking.com website that I tend to use and it was easy to see why the reviews were so favourable.

On arrival, we were greeted with a very warm welcome and the standard of accommodation was very good.

We ate in the restaurant and from the set menu which was priced at €20 for a three-course meal (which included half a bottle of decent wine), so at only about £14.50 or so each who could grumble?

I ate well and had the zucchini, stuffed with ham and cheese in a spinach sauce, followed by lasagne bolognese and then an almond tart of some description that was served warm and was particularly lovely.

The nearest description I can come up with for it was that it was like some sort of frangipane type pastry with an almond cream. I think it's a pretty traditional offering in the Basque Country, but whatever the proper description, it was excellent and satisfied my craving for something sweet.

The fact that the hotel turned out to be such a good place to stay rounded off what had been a great afternoons riding.

Sheep shit and ice

On Friday morning, the four of us met up around 08.00am and enjoyed a nice and plentiful breakfast.

We were packed and on the road for a little after 09.00am and after filling up with fuel we headed for Sort in the province of Lleida Catalonia.

Our route was to take us up into the Pyrenees and onto what was to become another excellent days biking.

We could have taken a much more direct route than we did but we were in no rush and so went with the route that Rich had planned in advance.

It's reasonable to say that Rich is something of a master when it comes to route planning and the effort he puts in in advance of a trip always pays off and this was the case again as we zipped along at a fine pace on fabulous roads, taking in some beautiful and amazing scenery that had plenty of mountains, gorges and rivers.

At the highest point on our route that day we were at about the 1,800 metre mark and were exposed to some odd weather conditions.

Much of Europe had been beset by untypical weather and we had a real mix as we climbed up into the Pyrenees.

It's worth a moment to reflect that the word 'sort', is Catalonian for luck but we certainly didn't feel lucky when still pretty high up, with cloudy weather and the feel of rain in the air we came across a piece of road that had the densest covering of sheep shit I have ever seen!

It was almost as though hordes of sheep had actively been encouraged to empty their bowels on a very specific patch of road.

I'm not kidding it was so bad that as well as it being potentially hazardous from a rider perspective it actually left us with sheep shit all over the bikes – it was even as high up as the Kriega pack that I'd strapped onto my back seat – and it smelt just as bad as you would expect.

As we continued to make our way, the weather turned, and even though I'd opted to wear textiles rather than leathers on this trip it was obvious that unless we stopped to put waterproofs on we were in for a right soaking.

I don't think I have ever seen weather change so dramatically and so quickly.

Within the shortest of times the sky had darkened, and what had started as rain almost instantly became hail, big enough and coming down hard enough for us to be able to feel it crashing against our clothing.

The nature of the road we were on meant that we couldn't pull up immediately but I was sure that Rich who was in front would pull up just as soon as it was safe to do so.

I was right and after a couple of minutes riding in what was becoming increasingly difficult weather we stopped at a sort of lay by just 150 metres or so before a tunnel through the mountains – it was to be a particularly fortuitous stop.

No sooner had we stopped than the heavens absolutely opened and we were covered by the most amazing dumping of hard hailstones that I have ever seen.

There was barely anywhere to shelter and we didn't hang about unpacking and getting our wet gear on, as well as changing from dark visors to clear visors.

It was so bad that it was actually quite difficult to walk without slipping and sliding on the covering of frozen ice pellets.

Just as we'd got our gear on I said to Col *"I'm not riding in this, it's un-rideable"* – and at the same moment as I had said it we saw a couple approaching the tunnel on a motorbike ... it was obvious the rider was struggling to maintain control in the dreadful conditions that had almost come out of nowhere.

It was a KTM 990 SMT and as valiantly as the rider tried, he just couldn't keep it up. He had done a great job of getting the speed down but he was riding on what was almost sheet ice and the inevitable happened and he went down.

Thankfully he was at a low speed and no doubt the covering of hail and ice on the road ended up helping to minimize damage and injury as the bike slid along with the rider and passenger underneath it.

Between us we signalled to traffic that there was an incident and helped lift the machine off the bikers and into a safe place.

I think the couple were Swiss, the rider spoke English but his partner didn't. He seemed OK but I suspect she had picked up some bruising and in any case, she seemed, quite understandably, to be in a mild state of shock.

Fortunately, the bike seemed to have only superficial and cosmetic damage and nothing that would stop them continuing their ride once they felt able to.

We ended up waiting around 45 minutes or so until the storm had eased and more importantly the ice covering the road had started to be washed away.

After checking with the Swiss couple that they were OK we set off, it was still raining but the road surface whilst not ideal was rideable with a degree of care.

Had we not stopped when we did and continued another 150 metres or so into the tunnel we would have come out the other side onto sheet ice and I wouldn't have fancied the chances of any of us staying upright – I think we had a lucky escape.

It didn't seem to take long until the weather changed again and we pulled over to take off our waterproofs before continuing to make our way on some wonderful winding and twisting roads towards Sort.

I recognized some of the places we passed and some of the roads we travelled on as I'd been down that way a few years ago on my own.

So in addition to enjoying the 'moment' I was also able to be reminded of some great memories from 2010 when my trip had included a journey through central Spain, down as far as the Douro Valley in Portugal and the Arribes del Duero Natural Park in western Spain before eventually heading to the area we were now in, then down via the Mediterranean coast and up to the Italian Lakes.

Sorted in Sort

The run into Sort was superb, fast paced riding on wide well surfaced roads surrounded for the most part by some fantastic scenery.

We stayed overnight at the Hotel Les Brases, an alpine styled hotel which is surrounded by wonderful views of the mountains and the Noguera Pallaresa river.

It was an easy enough place to find with it being pretty much on the main street through the town.

The hotel was more than acceptable for our stopover and with secure parking for the bikes in the hotel garage it ticked all the boxes.

Sort itself is a fairly small town in the province of Lleida in Catalonia and although it only has a population of around 2,000 or so it can be a busy and bustling place and is incredibly popular as something of an adventure sports centre and seemed to be well set up for camping, walking, kayaking and the like.

There is also a museum there that if I had more time I would have liked to have visited.

It was opened in 2007 and provides a memory of the almost 3,000 refugees who were fleeing from the Nazis across the Pyrenees and who were detained there for the duration of the war.

It's a great place to be on a bike, with a range of mountains, passes and lakes all close by and I reckon any biker would find plenty to excite them on the surrounding roads, not least a blast on the N260 that runs between Sort and La Seu d'Ugell.
To give it a geographical context, it pretty much borders Andorra and France and is around 200 miles from Bilbao, a little under 300 miles from Madrid and only 80 or so miles from the seaside city of Barcelona on the Mediterranean coast.

We drank in the hotel bar and ate in the hotel restaurant and all at excellent prices, helped of course at that time by the favourable exchange rate that sterling enjoyed against the euro.

As ever I was up early on the Saturday morning and took a walk around. It was the kind of location that would have been good enough to base ourselves for a few days had we wanted to stay in one place and had we not had other plans.

In terms of our accommodation then it's probably fair to best describe the hotel rooms as more functional than luxury but they were more than adequate for our needs.

Although the hotel was good value, in some respects it was also relatively expensive, and yes I know that's something of a contradiction but its slightly higher room rates are probably down to the basis of its location and perhaps the simple logic of supply and demand of Sort being something of an all year-round destination.

After our usual breakfast meet up and plenty of good humoured banter we had the bikes out of the garage, loaded and fired up and on our way around 09:00am.

The weather on Saturday was superb and it was good to be out in the warm sunshine, we were headed towards the south of France and the small village of Portal des Corbieres in the Narbonne district.

We didn't take the most direct route – had we done that we could have completed the day's journey in just a couple of hours.

Once again Rich had set out an excellent route and we really did have some stunning riding as we headed west away from the coast and for the Regional Natural Park of the Catalan Pyrenees.

It turned out to be another fabulous day and probably for about 90% of the day we were on roads that were devoid of traffic and roads that I reckon most any biker would rate as better than 8 out of 10

French hospitality

We arrived in Portal des Corbieres around 16.30 and the timing was perfect for our hosts as they were getting ready to dash off to a wedding that we'd passed as we'd entered the village.

We had made an effort to get there early as I'd been in contact with Jean-Luc and Bridgette (the owners of the hotel) a few times in the weeks running up to our trip and so was aware of their plans and their need to get off to the wedding service and reception.

On arrival, we were greeted by Bridgette who introduced us to Jean-Luc who was busily putting his tie on as he gave us a guided tour of what turned out to be super accommodation.

Despite the obvious rush that Jean-Luc and Bridgette were in to get to the reception, he took time to invite us to help ourselves to a bottle of wine at their expense and also to feel free to help ourselves to drinks in the fridge (beer, soft drinks etc) all priced at €1 with the money for any drinks taken to be left in a 'trust box.

The Relais De Tamaroque was better than good, in fact I'd describe it as different and exceptional and I would be more than happy to recommend it as a great place to stay if you are ever traveling down that way.

It's actually an old coaching house located right at the mouth of the River Berre.

All the rooms there have a view of the valley and all are furnished in that classic French way that many aspire to recreate in their own homes but few are able to achieve the genuine level of authenticity that we were set to enjoy.

It really would be a pretty ideal place to stay if you wanted to spend time exploring the Languedoc coast – but I reckon you wouldn't want to stay there if you didn't have your own transport to get about.

The place really is different and simply oozes French charm and even has a games room in what used to be the old stables.

With a pool table and table football to go at we were not short of something to do, although I should say that the table football provided some controversy as I was soundly beaten by Rich ... and I don't think I have ever seen three grown blokes want one other person to get beaten so much.

Something to do with being competitive I think, and yes it was me that was roundly beaten much to the pathetic delight of my travelling companions!

Before we used the games facilities we had a walk through the village and had a cold beer before wandering back and booking a table at a restaurant just two doors away from our accommodation.

The village itself is small with a population of around a 1,000 and we were bathed in the hot evening sunshine as we wandered around.

Once refreshed with a cold beer we took our table at a wonderful restaurant called Les Terrasses de la Berre.

It was a Saturday evening and the place was busy, which was sort of surprising given the empty stillness of the village we'd just walked through and I think we got the last remaining table.

Our hostess spoke English well enough to effectively translate the menu for us and the food was just as good as the first-class service we received.

The restaurant is only a hundred yards or so from the hotel and if you ever do get down to that area I'm sure you wouldn't be disappointed with the accommodation we stayed in or the restaurant we dined in.

I gather there are another two restaurants in the small village as well.

On Sunday morning, I took a short stroll through the village in the early morning sunshine before returning for breakfast in a room that was large, light and airy and that dazzled with its charm and character.

The walls were decorated with an intriguing range of art work.

The one that caught my eye was quite a large piece that seemed to be made of a series of glazed tiles with a woman reclining on a chaise longue and looking at an odd Picasso like face.

As attractive as she was the picture seemed to depict her with rather large toes, which made for a somewhat intriguing composition.

Breakfast was great, with plenty of coffee, delicious freshly squeezed orange juice, fresh bread, cheese, meat and a wide range of homemade jams and marmalades.

Had I been traveling by car then I would definitely have bought a few bits and pieces of the local products that were on display and for sale and that were produced by Jean-Luc and Bridgette.

They included, wines, jams and other comfits, but of course traveling across Europe for three weeks on a bike presents some limitations about just how much can be carried and packing bottles of wine and jars of jam no matter how tempting was simply out of the question.

After the excellent breakfast, we packed and set off in the general direction of the Mediterranean coast and the towns of Sete, Narbone and Nimes and our last full day of the four of us riding together on this trip.

To be honest it wasn't the best of riding but there again we knew this would likely be the case – being on the coast it was always going to be busy and there wasn't really a great route to get to where we wanted to go.

The weather was glorious and the temperatures were set to rise to around the 27C mark, and although the riding for most of the day could only really be described as average the decent weather and wonderfully blue Mediterranean sky' were some sort of trade off.

Not all the riding was average though and we did find some reasonable stretches of road as we moved away from the coast and into the national park area and towards the Camargue, a 'wetland' recognised to be of international importance.

In fact, the Camargue is vast and covers over 360 square miles with brine lagoons cut off from the sea and circled by reed marshes

By mid-afternoon we were heading away from the coast and stopped around 15:00 for lunch in the pretty looking walled town of Apt in the Cote d'Azur region.

In addition to enjoying a decent lasagne I made a mental note to try and call back there sometime as it looked a pretty interesting place to spend a few hours.

If you do get the opportunity to visit Apt, you would want to take the time to find the 'old town' which lies behind the walled buildings and is pretty much centred around the 11th century cathedral with narrow streets winding between houses and no doubt fascinating walks and picture perfect sights – it must be a joy to be there on market day.

After our late lunch, we set off on the final leg of our day's journey towards the French town of Digne les Bains set in the Provence region.

Unfortunately, Digne as it is simply known, is the town that earned some notoriety in March 2015 when the Germanwings flight 9525, on its way from Barcelona to Dusseldorf came down just a few miles from there, killing all on board and in so doing earning its co-pilot Andreas Lubitz a dubious place in the history books.

This final leg of the first part of the Road Trip was pretty reasonable as we rode the 60 miles from Apt to Digne in Provence, stopping only to stretch our legs and take some respite from the heat.

As we approached our destination Dave took the lead from me on the road as he was familiar with the area.

In fact, it was his friends Jean and Isabelle who were to be our hosts for the night and who would provide us with the warmest of welcomes in their most intriguing of homes.

The final road up to Jean and Isabelle's was interesting to say the least – we climbed to around 1,200m ending our climb on loose gravel.

The left turn into their property was so tight that we had to ride past, make a U turn in the church grounds, head back and then head directly up the final incline that veered off and upwards to the right.

Jean (who Dave had met many years ago when biking in France) came out to welcome us and in truth we could not have asked for a warmer welcome.

After being shown to our rooms, getting showered and then getting a very welcome cup of coffee Jean showed us round one of the most impressive and remarkable private garages I have ever been in.

I don't know all of his background but I do know that he has been around bikes all his life and has probably had more bikes than I have had hot dinners.

He currently does some business with Dave buying and selling old classic bikes and I think he does OK at it as well.

I know there was a period when he was co-owner of a motorcycle shop and I get the impression that he is a more than capable and competent mechanic.

The garage was truly remarkable and I can't find words to do it justice, but among the bikes he still has, there was the first bike he'd owned and it was the one that he travelled to Russia on as a youngster ... like you do.

Jean and Isabelle were warm and welcoming hosts who were happy to have us share their table, their food and wine which included a varied selection of quite interesting cheeses, some of them local specialties.

Jean also set a small bottle on the table that had a small wooden wolf in and that tasted a little like Grappa (and around 45% proof) ... but with more miles to cover the next day we each had only the smallest of shots of this fine drink.

I didn't sleep very well and woke early and was up showered and dressed for 06.00.

I took a walk outside and enjoyed the wonderful panoramic views in the early morning sunshine, before having a chat with Jean who was out with Toby his dog.

By the time the others were up Jean had prepared the table for breakfast which was simple and satisfying – steaming coffee, fresh bread and a variety of tasty preserves.

As Jean and Isabelle had other commitments we were loaded and ready to go for about 08:15am and set off to ride the first couple of hours together before we went our separate ways.

The initial part of our journey involved us making our way 1,200m down the mountain from Jean and Isabelle's place by first of all taking it pretty slowly down the gravel incline, then left towards and into the church yard, making a U turn and then making a steady descent on the narrow and loosely surfaced road and not picking up any speed until the surface had become firm and properly constructed.

Having made our way down the mountain Dave led us into the centre of Digne, which is itself almost 2,000 feet above sea level.

Once in the centre, and having rode along the particularly pretty tree lined boulevard that was the town's main road, we stopped for petrol before heading off and out across the river Bleone that flows south west through the town.

Digne itself would probably be worthy of a longer stay as it has quite a rich history and in relatively recent times (World War II) was occupied by Italy and then later the German Army before being liberated by the Allied Forces in 1944.

Although today was the day that we were set to go our separate ways, after heading out of Digne we rode the first couple of hours together and headed in the direction of the medieval town of Barcelonnete in the southern part of the French Alps.

Almost immediately on leaving the centre of town we were onto a good road the D900A.

The D900A is quite a narrow road and is actually part of the Alps Maritimes and located in the Provence Alps (Cote d'Azur), it's known as a balcony road which means one that is cut into cliffs and it's more than worth the effort to get there and ride it.

It's an impressive piece of road, well surfaced and winding between incredibly dramatic rock formations, some of which curved overhead and reminded me a little of the road that sweeps through the Tarn Gorge in Southern France and one that I've done several times in the past.

Although in truth, the overhanging rocks formations were more dramatic and impressive and this road was better surfaced and empty which for me gave it the edge over and above the Tarn Gorge.

Around mid-morning we found a convenient place to stop for coffee before we said our farewells and wished each other the best for the remainder of our respective trips.

Col and Dave were heading for an overnight stay in Baveno on the shores of Lake Maggiore. Baveno really is a pretty place and is one of over 50 small towns set around the stunningly beautiful Italian lake.

It's been a popular place for us in different ways really.

I first stayed there for a couple of nights back in 2010 when I was traveling on my own and then again in 2011 when a few of us had travelled down that way and across the Alps and stayed for a couple of days.

Then the following year (2012) a group of us had also stayed down at a place called Varrelo Pombio itself some 20 miles from Baveno and we spent time skirting the eastern side of the lake after crossing the bridge on the E62 before heading for the Swiss Alps via Belinzona, Biasca and beyond.

Later another biker friend Mick who had been forced to miss this trip because of health issues had returned there with his wife.

Earlier in 2015, just a few months before this bike trip my wife and I spent a few days down near Lake Maggiore when we'd driven down through Germany and then into Italy via the wonderful San Bernadino Pass in the Graubunden area of Switzerland.

So, you can see that in one way or another it's charms have been enough to call us back several times. It's a part of Italy for which I have many fond memories and if you've never spent time in that part of the Italian Lakes I can more than recommend it.

Lake Maggiore itself is a stunning lake and is around 65km (40 miles in length). Lake Garda has a greater surface area but Maggiore is actually the longest lake in Italy.

The lake itself is partially in Switzerland (Ticino) and a look at a decent map will show you the border between the two countries actually runs across the lake.

If a visit to the race track at Monza is your thing then it's a pretty convenient location for that as well, but having made the trip to Monza a couple of times I can't really recommend a trip there, as there is little to see and do (on a non-race day) other than see some of the old track and experience the simple joy of being there.

Time to go our separate ways

After an overnight in Baveno, Col and Dave's route would take them across the Alps via the Gothard Pass and onto their overnight stop in Germany and then on the last full day of their trip they'd booked to stay overnight in the pretty Luxembourg town of Vianden.

Their final day of this year's trip would then consist of the ride to Calais and travel back to the UK via the Eurotunnel.

Rich and I had other plans and we'd both booked accommodation for that evening, but after that it was pretty much a 'take it as it comes' type of trip.

Although we'd both booked accommodation in Italy we were going to different places and would head in separate directions later that day but we did share the ride together for the next few hours.

After the coffee stop and farewell's Rich and I headed across the Col de Larche.

The Col de Larche is a high mountain pass that rises to almost 2,000 metres (6,549') above sea level. Its route stretches between the Cottian Alps and the Maritime Alps.

It's a cracking good road and you are more or less on it after leaving Barcelonnette – the road is actually called the D900.

The upshot of starting the day on the D900A and then the D900 meant that we had some pretty fabulous riding and I would have no hesitation to say to bikers that it really is worth adding these to their list of roads to do if ever traveling in that area.

The weather and road conditions were magnificent with warm, smooth dark ribbons of tarmac set below the bluest of skies and bathed in bright warm sunshine.

This was truly a good moment to be on a bike on this most inviting of roads – quite simply it was a joy to ride.

Later Rich and I stopped for some lunch (we were now in Italy), and then headed towards the Piedmont area and the town of Alba.

Apparently, Alba is famed for white truffle, peaches and its wine production and although we didn't get to see or sample the truffles and peaches we did see plenty of vineyards.

For what it's worth Alba is also the home of the Ferrero confectionery group, that is now an international brand of some repute with production centres across the world.

It was shortly after our lunch stop that I noticed the 'bar end' on the right-hand side of the handle bar was working loose.

For those unfamiliar with a motorbike, a 'bar end' is essentially a weight that is attached to either end of a motorbikes handle bars and that works to reduce vibrations that can occur at certain frequencies.

It was a quick fix only requiring some simple tightening with an Allen key – in fact it took more time to stop and unpack the correct sized Allen key than it did to actually tighten it, and we were soon on our way again.

Over the years and whilst traveling it's true to say that I have seen some pretty extensive vineyards whether in Spain, Germany, France and Portugal but to be honest I don't recall ever seeing such extensive vineyards as I saw here as we travelled through the Piedmont area, an area from where one of my favourite red wines Barolo comes.

It was a remarkable and beautiful sight.

We stopped just outside our destination town of Alba so we could check maps and say our farewells.

It was gloriously sunny and very very warm and at the same time as I was sorry to say goodbye to Rich, in truth I was also hugely looking forward to Part Two of the trip on my own – and I'm pretty sure Rich felt like that as well.

6 - THE TRIP – PART TWO

It's great traveling by motorcycle with friends but there is also something quite different and quite good about traveling on your own.

Of course, it doesn't suit everybody – but you don't know how good it is, and liberating it can be unless and until you try it.

What if you don't break down

To be honest I have met plenty of bikers over the years who have said how much they fancy riding in Europe but who have allowed themselves to be put off by thinking about or being concerned about what might go wrong, what if the bikes breaks down and what if this and what if that and so on.

Whilst I can sort of understand those concerns my own rather simplistic view and that I have already mentioned is what if it doesn't go wrong and what if you don't break down?

But you know even if the bike was to break down or something was to go wrong, then whilst it might not be ideal or desirable, and it certainly wouldn't be part of your plan, then really it would just be the start of the next part of your journey and who knows where it might lead you?

If its security, organized comfort and a fixed itinerary that you want, then maybe it's best to stick to 'resort' type holidays – which have got their own place and I know suit many people for all sorts of reasons.

Some people are happy to be part of something organized and in fact there are many organizations that exist to provide organized holidays for bikers, which again is fair enough if that's what suits you – but it's not for me.

In the same way traveling to a soulless airport, sitting on a plane then spending a couple of weeks in a resort before heading back to another soulless airport etc etc doesn't really quite do it for me.

Although it can have its plus points i.e. being able to quickly get to somewhere, it doesn't really make the top of my list when it comes to travel.

I think traveling on your own can make you look at and appreciate things differently.

You do things in your own time and at your own pace, spending a couple of weeks at a resort type place might show on a passport that someone has **been** to Mexico, Spain or wherever but I don't think it always means that that person has **travelled** there.

It's horses for courses and all that so I'm simply offering an opinion rather than a judgement.

I suppose in a way maybe it's the difference between having a quick cup of instant coffee at home as opposed to sitting down in a coffee house and enjoying the rich taste and aroma along with the associated sounds and activities of the barista.

At the end of the day it's just a cup of coffee, but ... well you get my drift?

And then almost by way of contradicting what I've said I would always be more than happy to consider grabbing a cheap late bargain for a week in the sun somewhere – but grabbing a week in the sun and 'travel' are not always the same.

So there we had it Part One of the trip was over as Rich and I set off on our paths to each enjoy our own Part Two.

On my own

I was headed to a very small town called Bozzole. It wasn't a great distance from Alba, in fact the most direct route would have only been around 50 miles – but not for the first or last time on this trip I wasn't really interested in taking the most direct route.

Bozzole really is a small village with just some 300 or so residents and situated in Piedmont in the Province of Alessandria, about 50 miles from both Turin to the west and from Milan to the east and just a mile from Pomaro Monferrato, itself a small village with a similar population level to Bozzole.

And just to emphasise how small Bozzole is, it covers an area of less than four square miles.

I'd booked into a small place called Casa Mortarino and it was to prove to be a great stopover with a host as charming as the accommodation.

My host – Michaela had an excellent grasp of the English language, which maybe wasn't too much of a surprise when I learned that she had done a language degree in German and English at Milan University before working as a language translator in Germany for nine years.

It was whilst she was working in Germany that she met her husband Frank.

Michela and Frank had returned to Italy relatively recently to establish the Bed and Breakfast business by making their country home into an attractive six bedroomed Bed & Breakfast and holiday apartment place.

Michaela provided me with a warm welcome and in fact had dropped me a text message earlier in the day to ask whether or not I would like her to prepare me an evening meal – she really did provide a first-rate service.

The accommodation was lovely with a fine attention to detail in both design and quality.

The property has a large garden with table and chairs and all the other things you might expect to find in a garden in the summer ... plus a family of tortoises!

It had been another steaming hot day and after my warm welcome I had a much-needed shower and once cleaned up and refreshed I went for a walk around the village.

It was still around 25C so shorts and T shirt were just fine.

There isn't a great deal in the village of Bolzolle, but I did find a bar that although 'closed' had the door open and so I wandered in and the lady who was in there chatting to someone did serve me a bottle of beer and explained it wasn't actually open again until 9pm that evening.

One of the things that struck me as I wandered around the village was that it seemed that almost every residence had a dog of some description that barked like crazy as I went past – in fact my hosts had just acquired a new dog a week or so before I arrived there, and although I think he was from some sort of dog's home he seemed happy enough.

I couldn't help but think he was fortunate to have been adopted by such a decent person.

After enjoying the taste of the crisp cold beer, I ambled back to my accommodation and bought a slice of pizza and a bottle of beer from the only store in the village.

When I got back in, Michaela couldn't have been more helpful and offered to make me something to eat or drink but I was fine with what I had and my slice of pizza proved to be a more than adequate evening meal.

Breakfast the following morning was good, although my host was very apologetic about a delay in getting fresh bread to me.

She explained that there was no longer a baker in the village and she had to wait for it to be delivered – with this in mind she was thinking about learning how to bake bread so as to overcome this issue.

The breakfast was ample with ham, salami, a decent range of cheeses, some fruit juice, a couple of cups of coffee, and Michaela did indeed nip out to get me some fresh bread rolls.

After breakfast and after packing up we wandered together around the garden where she showed me the tortoises and also her father's 35-year-old moped.

She also told me she had taken a picture of my bike as her father had 'phoned to ask *"what bike the Englishman was riding"*.

After wandering to the end of the garden and anticipating my curiosity, Michaela opened one of the barn doors and took the covers off an old Vespa.

Although I can't claim to be any sort of knowledge on old scooters this one did indeed look something of a rarity with two separate seats, almost like the sort of seats that you might find on a pedal cycle.

I think this scooter had also belonged to her father Mario, but was in need of some restoration, which in the longer term is in the plans, but for now was a task that had to wait.

We chatted for a while and Michaela said she thought she had let me down as she had wanted to give me beer or sandwiches but explained that I had been so quiet when I came in.

I tend to sleep easily after a full days riding my bike which I guess was the explanation for my quietness, I'm hardly an all-night clubber at the best of times – but I did accept a bottle of water to take with me for my journey.

We continued to talk in general and I told her that my wife and I had been in Italy a few months previously and she added that if I return with Pat she would make up for not providing me with beer and sandwiches by giving us wine in the garden.

It was a generous offer that she really had no need to make, perhaps one day we will take her up on that.

She also told me about their plans for the country house and it all sounded fabulous, she was undoubtedly the perfect host and I would have no hesitation in recommending the Casa Mortarino as a wonderful and peaceful place to stay.

Heading further south

I was on the road for a little after 09.00am and headed south into Tuscany and a place called Carmignano in the Italian province of Prato.

I'd picked Carmignano for my next stop as it was in the general direction that I wanted to head and was only around 220 miles which seemed an ideal distance for lazy days riding though Tuscany.

It seemed to be a good enough location for an overnight stay, with a population of around 15,000 it's not a big place but with it being only around some 15 miles from Florence which I intended to visit, it fitted the bill.

I planned my route to take in a road called the SS45, as it was one that Rich had recommended to me in a text message the previous evening

Well what a recommendation it was – a wonderful road that more than ticked all the riding boxes, added to that was the glorious weather, which by midday was around 32 degrees.

The most obvious route to take would have been to head towards Genoa, but this wasn't really somewhere that I wanted to go.

With that in mind I made a point of turning away from the 'obvious' route and heading back into the hills and the wonderful tranquillity of the area and made my way to a town called Bobbio in a valley called Val Trebbia.

This is an area that was once described by author Ernest Hemingway as the most beautiful in the world.

He may have been right but I suppose I haven't seen enough of the world to make such a judgement – but in any case, it was truly beautiful and an absolute joy to be riding my bike in this area.

From Bobbio I dropped down towards Ascona then towards Santo Stefano d'Averto and then followed glorious shimmering roads to Bedonia with the towering Mount Pelpi to the north with its huge cross on the top to mark a religious miracle of the Virgin Mary.

Beyond that and a little to the west lies an even higher mountain Monte Penna – the best part of 6,000 feet high.

I had decided that I would go via Pisa and so continued my journey in the hills and mountainous areas.

La Spezia towards the coast had been recommended to me and although I had been tempted to head that way I just couldn't find it within me to leave the beauty and thrill of riding in the hills.

When I did get to Pisa I did the tourist thing and parked up in sight of the leaning tower and not surprisingly got a couple of pictures of it ... well come on what did you expect me to do?

I had enjoyed another wonderful day, and one that had been full of decent roads, but it had been a long day.

I was hot, sweaty and more than ready for a shower as I made my way to what I thought was the place I had booked.

It actually took me a little while longer, well much longer really, than I would have hoped to find my accommodation.

I arrived in a small village that had a very similar postal address but was actually about a dozen or so miles from where I needed to get to.

In fact, when I arrived at the place that I thought was my accommodation I took my bike down to what I assumed was the car park before realizing it wasn't a car park at all, which then gave me the rather difficult task of turning my bike around on a steep slope with a difficult camber.

The whole effort of getting the bike turned around left me in an even warmer state than I had been in and I was in desperate need of a cold drink.

An elderly lady and a young fellow, who seemed to be one of the workers at the place that I had wrongly thought was my overnight stop watched me struggle with some bemusement.

When I eventually got my bike back up the road and onto level ground they were helpful in giving me advice as to where I needed to go and at least if they thought I was a foolish traveller they had the good grace not to show it whilst I was there.

Although my accommodation was only a dozen or so miles on I decided to head back the way I'd come a short while earlier and back to a bar that I'd seen so that I could get myself a cold drink, and although hot and tired it wasn't really a chore as the switchback roads on the way were almost shouting for me to ride them.

The road really was a bit of a gem so it was no effort at all to do a few more miles.

One ice cold coke and a bar of chocolate later I made my way to my accommodation at Affittacemere Donati Nada which was actually a little further out of the wine growing town of Carmignano than I had anticipated.

After grabbing a shower and getting changed I made the three-mile round trip into town on foot and bought some produce from one of the local stores, which included buying some sort of bread with grapes in and which turned out to be very tasty.

Although my room could only really be described as adequate it did have a decent Wi-Fi connection and so later that evening I had FaceTime on my iPad to chat first with my wife and then later with my Mum and Dad.

I slept really well and was woken by my alarm at 07.00am and almost immediately got on with looking at the maps and planning my route for the day.

Breakfast was as basic as my room and in truth wasn't the best, but it was balanced out and compensated for by the friendliness and simple honesty of my hosts so no complaints from me.

I didn't spend much time checking out Carmignano it really had just been a stopover and I was on my way before 09.00am having decided that I would head for Florence then Siena and end my day in the Umbrian town of Orvieto.

Off to the walled city

The day looked like it would probably be one of the shorter riding days in terms of miles covered and it would allow me to amble along and spend some time later on exploring the walled city in Umbria, which looked fantastic when I checked it on the web the night before and was the key reason I had decided to head that way.

My visits to Florence and Sienna were only cursory visits really as they are far too special for me to visit without Pat.

Although we have not quite settled when we will travel there I do have an expectation that at some point we will see this magnificent part of Italy together and spend some time in Tuscany.

If that does work out, then Florence and Sienna are sure to be on our list as they looked to be the most beautiful of places.

My journey down to Orvieto was relaxing and easy.

The weather was hot and up around the 30c mark. Once out of Sienna it was easy traveling on the Tuscan roads under the blue skies and hot sun.

The roads were all but empty and I travelled a large stretch of my journey on a road called Casia.

At times it reminded me of parts of Spain that I'd ridden back in 2010 but with more colour, rather than the more parched and arid landscapes of northern Spain.

The smooth tarmac surface shimmered in the daytime heat and the roads just rolled off into the distance and really did provide for some pretty relaxed riding.

I had a very pleasurable and lazy stop at a roadside bar where I sat for what seemed an age, sipping coffee and coke and just enjoying the glorious sunshine and landscape.

The Casia road is of some historical significance and importance and leads north from Rome.

It has a history that can be traced back to the second century BC and was originally named after a Roman Consul (and so was known as a consular road).

Not for the first time (or the last) on this trip did I find my way somewhat indirectly to my accommodation. I had headed for Orvieto when I ought really to have headed to Orvieto Scalo.

But making the mistake of heading for the old town proved to be something of a bonus as I made my way up to what is truly a dramatic location set on top of volcanic stone (called Tufa) about a thousand or so feet above the floor of the valley.

When up there, the views across Umbria are just amazing. It's incredible 14th century Roman Catholic cathedral must be among the most impressive I have ever seen.

The cathedral is dedicated to the Assumption of the Virgin Mary with its outside walls really being something to behold – a visual feast of reliefs, statues and glittering mosaics – even to my untrained eye it seemed something of a masterpiece.

I rode slowly around the narrow streets long after I'd realized that I was in the wrong place. It seemed to be almost traffic free and I wasn't at all sure whether or not I should have been there on my bike but I just thought that I'd make the most of it in any case.

Eventually I made my way down and away from the old medieval walled town and into Orvieto Scalo.

The actual 'new' town is nothing special, and in truth I found it quite dull really.

I soon found my accommodation at the Hotel Picchio and after checking in put my bike in the underground car park, got showered, changed into T shirt and shorts, went for a refreshing cold beer in the hotel bar and then set off to walk the short distance to the funicular railway.

I took the funicular train along its 580-metre route, part of which is through a tunnel of over 100 metres cut through the rock and back up to the walled city, for a fee of about €2 return.

I was soon up at the top doing the full tourist experience – wandering around, snapping pictures and even enjoying an ice cream cone.

Once I had had my fill of the old town I made the short journey back down the funicular railway and decided it was time to get a bite to eat.

I had my choice of a number of pizzerias, all of which looked pretty ordinary – I opted for one for reasons that I can't recall and sat down in splendid isolation.

The service was good and I soon had a pizza cooked on a wood burning oven along with a half-litre of acceptable house wine and watched part of the Monaco v PSG football game that was being shown on the TV.

My evening meal and drink including tip cost me only €10, once again the location along with the favourable exchange rate were making for pretty low cost meals.

Back in my room I used the iPad again to have a FaceTime conversation with my wife Pat, but I was more than tired and shortly after our FaceTime conversation I was soundly asleep.

Breakfast at the Hotel Picchio was nice enough but I was keen to get going as my next stop would be Pompeii, some 240 miles away and where I had decided to stay for a couple of nights.

The ancient Roman town of Pompeii just a few miles from Mount Vesuvius was where I'd decided to base myself so that I would be well set for the Amalfi Coast. It also meant that I was another day closer to the undeniable pleasure of a clean pair of riding socks!

Pompeii and the Amalfi Coast.

I'd taken breakfast early at the Hotel Picchio which was probably just as well.

After collecting my gear from my room and calling to reception to check out, the small breakfast room that had been empty a short while earlier was now full and bustling with mostly Japanese tourists – there wasn't an empty table in sight.

It felt like a great morning to be on the road and once again the weather looked set to be wonderful with a stunning bright and clear blue sky overhead.

The roads out of Orvieto were first class and the air temperature was a glorious 33C by 11.00am.

Once again I was struck by the amount of space and the richness of the colours that surrounded me. Umbria was easy on the eye, and I was truly happy as I rode past olive groves, vineyards and hills topped off with Cyprus trees.

The empty and well-surfaced road I'd taken, dropped me down to the town of Bolsena located on the eastern side of the lake (with the same name) in northern Lazio.

A miracle was said to have happened there in the 13th century, which later led to the cathedral that I'd seen in Orvieto being built to commemorate it.

I stopped for a while to enjoy the tranquillity and to look down on the stunning views of the lake surrounded by the fairly low lying hills.

I carried on and then stopped again at Viterbo, the home of the Italian gold reserves before continuing onward and towards Pompeii.

It was going to be a long day and I decided that I would rack off a few miles on the Autostrada, which wasn't as bad as it might sound.

The lining had been out of my textile jacket for a few days and I was able to get some slight relief from the heat, but my forward motion wasn't generating cold air just an inward rush of warm air but it was helpful nevertheless.

In truth I made something of a mistake, as I hadn't planned carefully enough to give Rome as wide a berth as I ought.

The upshot of this was that I had a hot and messy journey through the outskirts of Rome, which seemed to take me ages and which was something of a challenge to survive intact.

As much as I think central Rome, and especially the historic area is truly deserving of being referred to as the eternal city, I had no interest in visiting Rome on this trip as I'd been there a couple of times in the past.

I've also been to, and driven in Naples before and knew only too well that central Naples was to be avoided at all costs on my bike.

I'm not sure what road I was on as I continued to make my way towards Pompeii, but at one point I recall being pretty surprised at the amount of open soliciting/prostitution.

I don't mean surpriscd from any sort of judgemental perspective, after all it's a fact of life and who am I to make judgements, but I was sort of shocked at what I saw.

There were prostitutes probably every 100 yards or so, sat on or stood by tired looking plastic garden chairs, many under parasols faded by the sun.

This scene stretched for maybe half a dozen miles.

At times these women who were plying their trade provided a stark contrast to the street advertisements that lined thc road.

Many of them stood below or in close proximity to these large advertising hoardings – many of which were selling someone else's aspirational dream of traditional white weddings and bridal wear along with the other things that go with someone else's view of what your money should be spent on.

Whilst I tried not to make judgements I couldn't help but think that this was more a case of needing to earn cash rather than a preferred lifestyle choice and the juxtaposition between the advertiser's world of happy ever after and the reality of street life seemed brutally stark.

A short while later I needed to stop for fuel and it was at this point that I had the one and only occasion of the trip when I felt a little uncomfortable.

It's quite common practice at Italian garages that an attendant will be on the forecourt to operate the pump, some take your payment on the forecourt (cash or card) and others direct you into the shop or forecourt booth to make your payment.

There were three men on the forecourt and no sooner had I taken my gloves off and pushed them under the handles of the panniers than they all moved over to where I was and one of them said no cards only cash.

Now it may well have been me being over anxious but it didn't feel quite right so I just got on my bike and went, gloves still tucked in the pannier handles.

I stopped a few hundred yards down the main road, put my gloves on and continued on to the next petrol station and filled up as normal. Maybe I misread the situation – who knows?

By the time I arrived in Pompeii the weather was very very hot and the temperature made the air feel stifling.

I had no trouble finding my accommodation at the Villa Flora which in fact was only 100m or so from the main entrance to the ruins.

In fact, the main road that my accommodation was on felt instantly familiar to me, as I had walked down there a few years back when Pat and I had taken the train from Sorrento to Pompeii where we had a great time doing the tourist thing around the ruins.

My room was of decent proportions and although the accommodation didn't provide breakfast the room did have a hob with two rings, a fridge and tea and coffee making facilities, which were ample for self-catering.

After grabbing a shower, I set off for a walk and decided that rather than eat out again I would call to a local Carrefour supermarket to get something to eat and drink for that evening as well as for breakfast the following couple of days.

There's nothing much to say about shopping at Carrefour after all one supermarket is much like another really, but it was cheap and I was able to buy enough food for two evening meals and two breakfasts as well as a bottle of wine and a couple of cans of beer for the sterling equivalent of around £14.

The Villa Flora provided acceptable accommodation as well as secure parking for the bike, and at around £58 for two nights provided terrific value as well.

The only drawback being that my room at the front of the hotel was noisy as there seemed to be traffic passing all through the night, which in turn meant that I didn't sleep as well as I would have liked to.

I was up early, made a good breakfast from the stuff that I'd bought the night before and was away from my accommodation for 08.30.

I turned left to make my way past the entrance to the Pompeii ruins and as I rode on the main road past the ruins, which was made out of large rectangular cobbles, it made me think that my bike would be in ruins as well by the time I got to the end of it.

It took me a while to get out of Pompeii; the roads were packed with folk on their way to work.

What did strike me that morning and then later in the day when I returned via Salerno, was what a full-on mess Pompeii is once you are away from the main drag and the pretty central square.

The back roads were rough, strewn with bags of rubbish and the place seemed to be in real stark contrast to what I'd seen of Italy on this and previous trips.

Living my dream

In many ways, the prospect of my ride today along the Sorrento coast road to Amalfi had been a key part of what first got me thinking about this trip.

A few years ago, my wife and I flew to Naples via Milan, hired a car and drove round the Bay of Naples to stay in the Grand Hotel Aminta in Sorrento.

The Hotel Aminta is in a fabulous location and looks out across the glorious Bay of Naples. We had a wonderful stay, and I suppose we did the things that many tourists do visiting Pompeii, Vesuvius and so on.

We also wandered to the public bus station in Sorrento and bought return tickets on the local bus service to Amalfi.

It was March time of year when we were there and the stunning coastal road was pretty empty.

On the way back I recall seeing a couple of bikes weaving their way up the coast road behind us until eventually they passed the bus we were on ... from that moment on I had determined that at some point I would have to return and do that road on a bike.

The immediate question of course, would be whether or not what lay ahead would live up to my hopes and expectations or whether I would be left disappointed.

After riding through Bano do Pozzano I headed down the SS145, the coast road towards Vico Equense before turning to head into the hills and found myself passing a restaurant/bar that had views that looked particularly inviting.

It was an ideal place to stop for what had now become my regular roadside order – a coffee and a glass of coke.

I sat in splendid isolation for a while looking out across the Tyrrhenian Sea and the island of Capri.

It really was pretty much perfect and I took a moment to drop Pat a text to let her know where I was and to thank her as well.

It wasn't so much that I needed to thank her but I didn't want her to think that I took this, or indeed any of my trips for granted.

Refreshed from my drinks and the most perfect of vistas I headed down the mountain to pick up the road into Sorrento.

Not surprisingly Sorrento itself was busy and sparked a few memories as I passed the orange trees that we'd walked under together some years previously, as well as seeing the road that led up to the Hotel Aminta.

It became apparent to me as I rode out of Sorrento – initially on the SS145 towards San Pietro and then the SS163 into Amalfi – that I was not going to be disappointed.

I was in my element – a simple mixture of being excited and challenged by the road.

Traffic was mixed really, in some stretches there was plenty, in other stretches there was none to interrupt the flow.

The views rank right up there, it really is stunning.

I've read in the past that it has been rated as one of the ten most beautiful roads in the world and whilst I can't validate that one way or another, it is unquestionably astounding and to be honest I would rate it as a 'must see/must do' sort of a road.

It's not without its risks and the nature of the road means that the buses and tour coaches can at times take the full width of the road as the drivers skilfully navigate the route.

The road is thrilling with its zigzagging tarmac and hairpin bends, the landscape is sensational, the colours amazing and the overall experience is dramatic and one for the memory banks if not for the faint hearted.

Every corner seemed to provide another breathtakingly beautiful view and a real benefit of being on a bike as opposed to being in a car or coach is that there are plenty of places where you can pull up and take photographs.

There were a few times though where I stopped simply to draw breath and take in the views.

Amalfi itself was rammed, as was the last mile or so into it and from a biking perspective was as joyless as it was pointless, but I carried on from Amalfi towards San Cosma, Minori and Ercha and onto Salerno.

The decision to carry on was the right one as it was more of the same road (SS163) but on this section, there was next to no traffic.

I had filled my boots and had only two 'moments', one when the front wheel had locked (my own carelessness) and another when the rear tyre lost traction and slipped, my increased heartbeat and buttock clenching were only momentary as the tyre gripped – but I must admit I did temper my speed for the next few corners.

I wasn't interested in sightseeing in Salerno – I'd come here to ride, but I did need a cold drink and rather than head into the city I dropped off into the docks and stopped at the equivalent of a greasy spoon for dock workers – and had my coffee and coke for just a couple of euros.

My journey back to Pompeii from Salerno was dull by comparison to my journey there but it was sort of interesting to see another part of that area – but as with my outward journey, when I got back to the outskirts and then the back streets of Pompeii it was nothing to write home about, and as I have already said a real contrast to so many other parts of Italy that I'd seen on this and previous occasions.

Back at the Vila Flora I had FaceTime with my wife and then later my daughter and grandchildren, before taking a shower to freshen up from the exertions of the day.

Later I walked into Pompeii, called to Carrefour for some anti Mosquito stuff as I'd been *'attacked'* on several occasions on this trip and then called at a bar for a large beer and a decent cup of coffee.

Whilst I sat outside I jotted down a few general observations, and have retrieved them from an email that I sent home. They were:

- Fiat 500 cars look just right on Italian streets in a way they don't at home;

- Italian people must be some of the most expressive with the use of their body language when talking (shouting) with each other;

- much of the impatience expressed seems to me more because it's what they do than with any real impatience, throw hands up, beep horn, shake head etc;

- the law on the use of mobile phones whilst driving is flouted beyond belief that makes the UK look compliant – frankly it's more than alarming. People text and read their mobile 'phones even on their scooters. The police openly ignore it, which makes me think it's openly condoned;

- Its ok to smoke when riding a motorbike or scooter – odd but OK;

- Italians are cool and have style in the most understated way. Men on scooters in suits with daft crash helmets seem to pull it off. Young women on scooters seem impossibly chic and stylish. An old man in full wedding suit including carnation buttonhole hurtling through traffic on his scooter in Pompeii didn't look at all out of place;

- there seems a full-on sense of chaos but everyone seems to know how they fit into that chaos;

- Italians use their car horns because they have them;

- Pompeii is not an attractive place once off the main drag nor is the 10 miles or so of the Route National from Salerno back into Pompeii streets. It's piled high with rubbish, the most remarkable levels of fly tipping but they do pick up dog muck;

- much of the back-street areas are more like a shanty town in this part of Italy;

- driving is risky in the towns;

- the seatbelt law is widely flouted;

- children were frequently sat in the front on the knees of adults;

- three on a scooter (mum dad and child) is common place;

- a frequently signed rule on the Sorrento/Amalfi coast road is to *give way to overtaking traffic*;

- coach drivers are pretty good with bikers waving you past when they know you want to get a shift on;

- coming around bends on the wrong side of the road seemed to be commonplace;

- petrol stations are satisfyingly inefficient with the number of people employed (even though I can actually put my own petrol in) ... but I like the fact that it must be giving people jobs;

- the south of Italy seems relatively poor – sweeping generalization I know but …

- Italy is the most wonderful of places.

After jotting down my observations, I ambled back to the hotel and fell asleep listening to some Tracy Chapman music that I had really taken to on this trip.

A lucky escape

The following morning (Saturday) I'd resolved to make an early start and I was on the road for just after 08.00am.

Another hot day was forecast and there were cloudless blue skies. Getting out of Pompeii was awful and unfortunately it wasn't without incident.

Weaving through the small streets was demanding and even though it was fairly early and there was less traffic on the road than the previous couple of days the driving standards seemed just as loose.

My approach whether around Rome, Florence, Sienna and now Pompeii had been to make a point of keeping my dark visor up and open so that I could make eye contact with drivers, this worked reasonably well but of course it gave no certainty of safety.

It was as I was slowly and carefully making my way through the back streets of Pompeii that a transit type van hurtled around the corner of a T junction,

I could see immediately that the driver had both arms resting on the top of the steering wheel and was using his mobile phone with both hands … it looked to me that he was going to hit me.

He certainly hadn't seen me and was oblivious to his surroundings.

I braked full on, brought the bike to a near stop but couldn't hold the weight as the front wheel of the bike slid slightly and then 'tucked' under on the Pompeii slab like surface.

I toppled over onto my left-hand side, thankfully this was at a low speed, in fact I suppose it was almost at zero miles per hour, but nevertheless the bike was on top of me.

An Italian couple in the car behind seemed to get out immediately and helped me lift the bike up.

It took a moment to find level ground to get the footrest down such was the unevenness of the street surface.

I was fine, they cussed in that typical Italian way and seemed to be cursing the driver, the word idiot along with plenty of demonstrative hand gestures were hurled at the driver of the van who carried on blissfully unaware.

As it had been such a low speed topple, it seemed the damage was minimal.

The left-hand mirror had folded in but was undamaged, the left-hand indicator had come off its rubber mounting and partially popped into the fairing.

Apart from that the bike looked to be intact other than a small scratch about one cm long on the left lower faring and which I didn't notice until later on.

I was left pretty uncomfortable for the afternoon and evening from having the weight of the bike on top of me but that was about it.

An unloaded Kawasaki Z1000SX weighs a little over 500llbs (230Kg), with luggage it clearly weighs more so it was little wonder that I felt stiff and sore for some time afterwards.

Other than stopping near a wonderful triple layered bridge to make a temporary repair to ensure the indicator wasn't going to work loose I carried on my way.

I had another incredible day and once I'd cleared Pompeii it was a climb into the hills through areas and roads that reminded me of Swiss alpine towns and then through open stretches that reminded me of some of the plains of Aragon in northern Spain.

Riding a bike gives you such a different experience than driving a car.

I don't want to get too flowery and ramble on about being in touch with nature but there really is something good about having your senses worked differently.

Whether it's the sounds and the sights seen from a different perspective or the interesting smells that you pick up as you flash through open spaces or make your way at a slower pace through towns and villages. All of these can often combine to give an all-round experience that maybe is like adding another dimension to your travel and just like you have a memory bank of things you've seen; motorcycling can give you a memory bank of things and places you've smelt and that sometimes come back to you at the most unexpected of times.

And sometimes there are single moments that can last just seconds or minutes sometimes stretching into hours where despite everything going on around you, or maybe even because of it you can experience a peacefulness and stillness that sets you apart from everything and everyone and at the same time as leaving you relaxed and fulfilled it can also leave you wanting so much more.

I suppose it's an addiction.

Heading for the Adriatic

Today was one of those days that was satisfying beyond belief and I set off leaving the Mediterranean coast behind me and headed towards Campobasso with a route that took me into the Matese mountains, across the Apennine's and then after reaching Campobasso dropping down and onto Termoli on the Adriatic coast.

At times the roads felt pretty perfect and as I travelled across the Apennine Mountains they were largely empty with the smooth dark tarmac twisting and shimmering in another baking hot day

Although I had marked Termoli on my map it wasn't where I planned to stay that night but it was a good point to aim for as I just wanted to get to the Adriatic coast.

Termoli was about five miles or so from where I planned to stay on Saturday night.

It's a biggish sort of a place with a population of around 32,000 and although the history books show that people have settled there since prehistoric times it wasn't until after WWII that it really began to expand.

It was the sight of one of the bigger tank battles of the Italian campaign during the second World War and used to be a fishing port of some note but is now much more of a holiday destination popular with Italians and somewhat unknown to non-Italian tourists.

Once I'd reached the coast I stopped on the sun kissed promenade for some time to enjoy the sunshine and the views of the Adriatic and took a few pictures of my bike, framed by palm trees and with the impossibly blue waters of the Adriatic as the most pleasant of backdrops.

Despite the exertions of the days riding I felt relaxed, refreshed and happy and eventually I made my way to my overnight accommodation in the hill top town of Campomarino in the Molise region and just a few miles south east of Termoli.

I'd made a booking at the Resideza Glave and had it not been for my further plans this was somewhere I would have been happy to stay for a few days.

My accommodation was pretty much in the centre of Campomarino in a superbly restored period building.

It was one of those places that I knew would be good as soon as I checked in, I couldn't have asked for a warmer welcome from my hosts they were just superb.

My bike was soon safely put away in a huge garage and I wasted no time in getting a shower. I went for a wander around the small town and walked amidst houses richly decorated with murals that completely cover them and that fill the streets and depict old and ancient crafts – it's a pretty place to visit.

The early evening temperature was still in the 30s and I stopped for an ice-cold beer at the first small bar I came to.

I had no plans for the evening and was in no rush to do anything at all, so simply did no more than sit outside the bar and while away the time with the simple enjoyment of people watching in the warmth of the evening sun and reflecting on the days ride and my journey so far.

Later I ate well at a small but superb restaurant - the Trattoria da Nonna Rosa just a few minutes' walk from where I was staying.

Here the owner himself cooks the food with something of an 'Italian flourish' – the place was good, the food delicious and with service to match there was nothing more I could ask for.

I was in bed and asleep for 9.30pm, way too tired to look at maps or think about the following days ride, which I had decided would be to Slovenia for a couple of days.

Off to Slovenia

I'd slept really well in very comfortable accommodation and after showering, getting dressed and making myself a drink I walked the short distance to get my bike from its overnight parking place in the rather large garage.

My host Gianfranco, had given me the remote control for the garage door and in no time at all my bike was back outside the accommodation and ready to be loaded up.

Before going down to breakfast, I packed my luggage and clipped the panniers to the bike.

I had a seriously good breakfast taken al fresco in the sun-drenched courtyard. Gianfranco and his wife Laura couldn't have looked after me any better.

The courtyard/garden really was a lovely place to have breakfast and I can't recommend this place highly enough as an excellent place to stay – whether as a stopover or for a longer stay.

It's even pretty close to the beach at Campomarino Lido on the Adriatic coast if that's your thing.

I looked at maps and checked distances on the Sat Nav whilst I ate breakfast and enjoyed a couple of excellent cups of coffee.

I made the decision to head to Slovenia for a couple of days, but would definitely need to stop somewhere overnight en route.

I'd decided that I would head to a place called Sigillo some 20 miles or so from Perugia for that mid journey stop.

After breakfast and before leaving, I borrowed a small screwdriver from my hosts so that I could tighten the screw that was holding the left-hand indicator in place – a small and very amateurish sketch of a screwdriver and the use of Google translate were helpful with that request.

There are actually two screws that hold the indicator in place on its rubber mounting brackets and although I'd managed to make a temporary repair after leaving Pompeii I hadn't been able to get the screw in as tight as I'd wanted.

The small screwdriver that I borrowed was just the job and allowed me to make a fix that I knew would be fine until I was back home when I could do the job properly and would be able to re-fasten the second and more awkward to reach screw.

I had some pictures with Gianfranco and Laura and then was on the road for around 09.00am – this was actually a little later than I'd intended because there had been internet connection problems and the owner hadn't been able to process my payment … but rather than delay he offered to do it later so as I could get on my way.

I started with the short journey back down to Termoli and then pretty much just followed the coast road to the town of Pescara which is about 60 miles away.

Along the way I couldn't help but be distracted by the perfect views to my right and on more than one occasion I stopped to take pictures.

After that I switched the Sat Nav on and headed inland for the town of L'Aquila in the Abruzzo region, about another 60 or so miles on from Pescara on the Adriatic coast.

This certainly wasn't the most direct of routes to where I was headed for the night but I went that way for no other reason than it being located close to the highest of the summits in the Apennine mountains and so it followed that the roads would be decent and the route exciting.

Although I'd only covered around 120 miles by the time I got there it'd taken me some time and a good few hours more than an equivalent route on less mountainous roads – but just like most other days on this trip I was in no rush, had no one else to think about and had no fixed deadlines.

After taking refreshments and a break in L'Aquila I pointed my bike in the general direction of Terni in the Italian region of Umbria, but not before making yet another mental note that this place looked worth coming back to.

There seemed to be so much more there than I could take in on a refreshment stop.

I had in mind that I would then go on to my evenings destination via Assisi and Perugia.

Terni itself was a good stretch from where I was, in fact it was the best part of another 100 miles to this fairly modern type of city with its old and ancient central area that dates back to the 7th century.

Interestingly there is also a connection to my home city, in so much as it was an important place in the 'second industrial revolution' in Italy and has been nicknamed the 'Italian Manchester'

I didn't go into Terni itself but skirted the city and headed towards Spoleto and then Trevi on the SS3, which was for the most part a main road but was helpful to ride on and to rack off a few miles.

The weather had been good again and very warm, around the 26/27C mark, but was set to change and despite starting the day in glorious weather, by early afternoon the sky in front of me was darkening and the weather looked ominous.

The strange weather that Europe had experienced several times throughout 2015 was back, and the rain started to fall.

I pulled over to swap to a clear visor and get my wet gear on.

The conditions were so bad that it didn't make much sense to continue to ride and I pulled over at the first roadside café I saw, and made the most of this enforced stop with a good cup of coffee, and sheltered for the next 30 minutes or so until the rain had eased.

Whilst having this coffee I dropped Pat a text message to let her know that she shouldn't worry if I was late making contact that night and that as conditions had changed I wouldn't now be taking in Assisi or Perugia but I would probably take a more direct route to Sigillo.

But wouldn't you know it – literally within 10 minutes of setting off the clouds cleared, the sun was out and it was time to stop again to get the wet gear off … and already I was way too warm.

The change in the weather was so dramatic that I decided that I would make the most of the now decent weather and head for Perugia but Assisi would have to wait for another time.

I was so glad that I made the journey to Perugia. If you're not familiar with the geography, then Perugia is about 100 or so miles north of Rome and about 90 miles east of Florence and is in, what I think is a very special part of Italy.

It's actually the capital city of Umbria, which in turn is bordered by Tuscany, Lazio and Marche.

I was able to ride around the old town and it's not an overstatement to say it's quite stunning.

Perugia is also famed as a significant seat of learning as a university town and in fact there is more than one university located there.

Although I was able to ride around the ancient town, leaving it was not without some peril as I inched down the steepest incline that I have ever gone down on a bike.

It was less than ideal as it was a mix of cobble type stones and concrete and I was glad and somewhat relieved to get onto the main road.

After leaving Perugia I headed for Sigillo some 30 miles or so away.

Heading up the mountain

I was heading for my accommodation at the Albergo Ristorante and had looked on Google Earth that morning and sort of knew what I was looking for, although the postal address was Sigillo it was actually a little way out in the Monte Cucco Natural Park in the Appenine mountains of the Ranco Valley.

As I got closer to my destination I was on brilliant roads that seemed as though they were trying to tie the bike and me in knots as they rose up and curved back on themselves time after time – despite it being a long long day on the bike I was quite simply in my element.

Eventually I reached the town of Sigillo and turned right for Monte Cucco.

The road ahead looked to have some steep sections and in parts was quite poorly surfaced.

From the base of the mountain towards the top was around three and a half miles and over that distance I would ascend some 1,200m.

Once I was pretty much at the top it looked to me as though I needed to take a sharp left to reach the Albergo Ristorante but the road looked like a loose gravel track that a 4×4 might have coped with but it wasn't one that I was prepared to even attempt.

I decided that it couldn't possibly be right so rode on a few hundred yards, turned the bike around, dismounted and then walked a little to see if I could see any possible sign of life or activity – I could see none.

I'm generally pretty relaxed when I'm travelling but I was a little concerned at this point as the light was fading, my fuel reserve light was on and I was 1,200 metres up a mountain not really at all sure of where I was and wondering had I made a big navigational error.

I reasoned that I must have taken the wrong turning and that it couldn't possibly be this high up and/or this isolated. So despite having checked this in the morning on Google Earth I decided I must be wrong and so picked my way back down the mountain.

I eventually got back down and asked the first people that I saw, who confirmed that it was indeed back up the mountain.

I asked them about the gravel/shale road I'd seen and they told me that if I carried on I would see signs for the Ristorante.

I was too low on petrol to attempt to go back up there so tapped the Sat Nav for the nearest garage and headed off there to fill up.

None of my credit cards were accepted in the automated machine but thankfully I had a €20 note which almost filled the bike up.

It was now dark as I headed back, but this time, the darkness allowed me to see lights high above me, which had to be the place I was looking for.

I made my way up pretty slowly, the first run in the falling light had given me a clue about the road surface and

I knew there were some bad patches as well as the need to look out for rocks on the road.

The second run up the mountain presented me with the additional bonus of a large white cow on the road but it wasn't at all interested in me and I passed close by it without incident.

So once again after a little over 3.5 miles and about 15 minutes I was back at the top and this time was able to find the place. I cursed myself for giving up first time.

The place looked to be very very quiet but looked good.

The Albergo Ristorante was different and bigger than I'd expected.

It also looked like it was past its heyday, and although perfectly fine it was a little old fashioned and the rooms would have benefitted from a makeover/update.

But I received a warm welcome when I arrived there and my bike was secure, I had a bed for the night, the restaurant was open and the food smelt good – what more could a biker want after a long day on the road?

After getting showered and changed I made my way for something to eat which I think was at about 20.45, they served until 21.30 so I had plenty of time and had a really nice meal, ravioli bolognese as my primi pasti and then a nice pizza with two glasses of red wine and all with excellent service.

After my evening meal, it was FaceTime with my wife, albeit it with a fairly slow and intermittent internet connection and then it was bed.

To be honest I didn't sleep too well and woke a few times with pains in my arms, wrists and hands.

The legacy of a biking accident in 2010 was making itself known again and the constant use of brake, clutch and throttle for the last dozen days or so was taking its toll.

I was up packed and ready for breakfast by 08:00, but in truth it was quite a contrast to Saturday's breakfast, it was acceptable but a bit more on the basic side than what I had become accustomed to for most of this trip – but the coffee was good and I had plenty of that.

When I checked out, the owner who was a really pleasant man was keen to know where I was going and where I'd been, his English was very good and he wished me well for the rest of my journey.

On the road to Slovenia

Today was the day that I would make for Slovenia and I'd decided to stay in the small town of Kobarid.

Kobarid is in the westernmost part of Slovenia and as such is within the Julian Alps, has a population of around 1,500 and is located in the Soca Valley.

I had never been to Slovenia before which probably was the single biggest reason I'd decided to go there.

It was also the town that Ernest Hemingway described in his book A Farewell to Arms as *'a little white town with a campanile in a valley'* and *'with a fine fountain in the square'* – but I have to report the fountain is no longer there or at least I couldn't find it.

The odd weather continued and as I left the Albergo Ristorante and made my way off the mountain I'd seen that the sky was darkening behind me and indeed it caught up with me after about an hour and I stopped to put on my rain gear ... thirty minutes later it was dry and bright and around 27C so another stop to take off the rain gear and then for almost all of the rest of the day, the weather was good again.

I knew in advance of leaving the Albergo that it wasn't going to be the best of rides – no matter which way I held the map up it looked a bit of a dull ride and for the most part it looked to be away from the mountains and hills and across the 'flatlands' of the Gulf of Venice, which borders Italy, Slovenia and Croatia.

I headed in the general direction of Trieste. I could have headed for the coast and sort of gone up via San Marino, but instead I opted to stay in the mountains a while longer and so headed first towards Gubio and then Citta di Castello and this way I knew I could probably get the best part of a couple of hundred miles or so before it all got a bit flat.

My route took me towards Bologna but I dropped down below that so as to avoid the city, I still had a fair way to go, today was a long day (the best part of 400 miles) and the second half of the journey was pretty much as expected and for the most part rather dull.

There isn't really a great deal I can find to say about my ride, other than I went on one particular road that was probably the longest and straightest road I have ever been on and which I think was the SS14 that runs towards Palmanova.

The SS14 was interspersed with two of the biggest and most bizarrely oversized roundabouts I have ever been on and only seemed to serve as a break to the monotony of the road to Udine.

As I approached my destination the weather darkened again and it looked like it might rain, I slipped my rain jacket on over my textiles just in case, but the rain held off, although it had clearly rained along the latter part of my route before I got there.

The town of Udine had received something of a drenching.

From there it was only around 40 miles to my destination but the air had definitely turned cooler.

In fact, had the roads not been so damp it would have made for superb riding as I made my way on very good roads into Slovenia and alongside the Soja river ... which was a raging torrent.

The water seemed to be more brown than aqua and that along with debris on the road was evidence that there'd been some pretty heavy rainfall in that area earlier in the day.

The damp roads and the debris made the only sensible option being that of riding the rest of my journey at a cautious and moderate pace.

My timing turned out to be just right, because as I pulled into the car park of the Fedrig s Prenocisci hotel the heavens absolutely opened, with rolling thunder not too far away.

A young lady came out to meet me and suggested I bring my bike in undercover and she helpfully moved some chairs so that I could put the Z1000 undercover and between some tables in the outdoor seating area.

The Fedrig s Prenočišči hotel was really very good and superb value.

When I was booking it online I saw that I could book a deluxe double room for less than €60 (a little less than £44) for two nights and this also included breakfast.

My room was spacious, had a balcony, solid wooden parquet floors and the bedroom was complete with bearskin rug and a very solid Wi-Fi connection.

After the usual shower and change, although this time not into shorts, I borrowed a large umbrella from reception and went for a walk.

By now the rain was hammering down, along with crashing thunder and a lightning storm that was so vivid and constant it was almost lighting the place up like daylight.

The young lady at reception who had greeted me (and who was the daughter in law of the owners) told me that they had endured a colossal amount of rain that day, she also explained that she thought it was quite localised but wasn't set to change anytime soon.

It only took me a minute or two to walk into the centre of the town and I noticed that there was a museum there that I decided I would visit the following day if the weather was still so bad.

After establishing my bearings, I took a beer and bite to eat in a small bar before making my way back to the hotel.

The thunder and lightning storm continued for most of the night.

Unlike the weather the following morning, the breakfast was good. I decided that I'd go for a walk and hope for a break in the weather later on in the day.

By the time I'd got my things together to go out the rain had stopped, but the clouds were low, the sky was grey and the surrounding mountains were obscured by the low hanging cloud base.

You can always learn something new

Kobarid is certainly a small town and in truth was a place I had never heard of until I decided to stay there and yet it has its own place in history.

It was here that various battles took place, including the Battles of Isonzo between Italy and Austria/Hungary.

One of the bloodiest conflicts of World War I happened there when Austrian troops supported by Germans broke through the front lines, and it's this chaotic period that is recounted in Hemingway's Farewell to Arms.

The museum that I'd seen the previous evening recounts all of this, and the poor weather had at least afforded me the opportunity to visit it and in my opinion is a 'must do' visit if you ever decide to stay and/or travel in that area and is great value for the €5 entrance fee.

It was fascinating and incredibly well presented; in fact, it was voted Best European Museum for 1993.

The (Kobariski Muzej) tells a moving story of incredible hardships and incredible loss of life – and made me think about the madness and futility of war.

In the Battle of Caporretto alone the figures were breath-taking, 10,000 killed, 30,000 wounded, more than a quarter of a million taken prisoner – and all this in less than a month.

By the time I'd done in the museum the weather looked decent enough – still grey and chill, but no rain and nothing to put me off getting on the bike.

Dodgy road conditions

The weather looked better back towards Italy rather than further into the Soca valley, and having gone out on the bike I turned off the main road at the first opportunity and took a smaller road up into the mountains, but it soon became pretty obvious that this wasn't going to be great and brought with it an element of risk.

In places the road was strewn with stones, rocks and mud that had been swept down from the storms of the previous night.

I'd read on the news that morning that the untypically severe weather – apparently, a rare Mediterranean storm that had crossed northern Africa - had also hit parts of northern Italy and was so severe there were reports of loss of life with flash flooding and mudslides.

My experience was just a mild taste of that but it was enough for me to decide not to press on that way, so I turned and headed back down to lower ground before heading south and back into Italy where remarkably and within less than 20 miles it was blue skies and sunshine and 27C.

On my way, I stopped and parked my bike in a clearing near the Soja river whose waters were now more like the aqua colour I had expected as the river had subsided a little after its drenching.

It was here that I met and chatted to four Germans who were changing into wet suits and preparing for a day's canoeing – other than that I just enjoyed the solitude and isolation of the moment.

The rest of the day turned into a sort of lazy riding day as I ambled around Italian villages and back roads, stopping to take pictures and then refreshments at a couple of small village bars.

My next to last stop of the day was in Udine where the temperature was now 29C. I made my final stop of the day at a supermarket on the way back to call to buy deodorant, but also ended up buying a gift for each of my two grandchildren.

Once back at the hotel and before dinner I decided to go for a walk and headed up a hill through a forest to the Sacario dei Caduti di Caporetto.

The monument and chapel at the top were built in memorial to the Italians who lost their lives in the battle that I referred to previously and as well as being a sombre reminder to the loss of life it also afforded wonderful views of Kobarid and the surrounding valleys.

Not only that but it provided a view of a road that I decided I would take the following day.

Back at the hotel I ate in the restaurant and enjoyed a couple of glasses of decent Merlot priced at just €0.85 a glass.

Next it was some route planning before bed and a very sound night's sleep.

Before going to sleep I'd decided that after breakfast I would head to the small village and ski resort of Madonna di Campiglio in the Trentino province of northern Italy.

There were a number of options for the route, the shortest being around the 220-mile mark or a longer route that although closer to 300 miles would be sure to take me much longer as it would involve heading into the Julien Alps, the Parco natural Tre Cime, the Dolomites and the mountainous area that went with it and then west towards the South Tyrolean Province of Bolzano, before dropping back south towards the Trento area.

My final decision would be weather based – what I didn't know before I went to sleep was that the following day was going to provide me with what was probably one of the best days I have ever had on a bike...

Maybe the best day on a bike ... ever

I slept later than planned but still managed to be away by around 09:15am.

At breakfast, there was only one other person in the room and it was obvious when she was asked what she wanted to drink that she was not a local, in fact she was Welsh.

She asked me was it my bike outside – given that I had my textile trousers, bike boots and a candy line green tee shirt that matched my candy lime coloured Kawasaki, then she was on reasonably safe ground in asking if the single bike in the car park belonged to me.

She told me that her brother, who she was traveling with, had been admiring my bike the previous evening.

Shortly after we'd made our introductions her brother joined her at the breakfast table and the three of us soon struck up an easy conversation.

It turned out they ran their own company (connected to medical supplies) and they used a manufacturer based locally in Kobarid.

It also turned out they were from my parent's home city of Cardiff South Wales – yet another example of the *'it's a small world'* type conversation. As with others that I'd met they wished me well for the rest of my travels.

I knew I had a long day ahead of me as I planned to ride to Madonna di Campiglio in Northern Italy.

The town is around 1,500 metres above sea level and is in the Brenta Dolomites in the Trentino region. I don't ski and have never had any interest in doing so, but apparently, this place is the number one ski resort in Italy with 57 lifts and some 150km of ski runs.

That sounds decent to me but as I've said I don't ski so can only really go on what I'd read in that respect.

As an aside and perhaps of interest to car and bike enthusiasts is that it's the location that the Ferrari Formula One team and the Ducati Moto GP team hold their media events in January of each year.

With my bike loaded and my end destination in mind I felt uncertain about the route I should take.

The clouds were low and the roads damp. The weather didn't look promising and I was also mindful of potential road conditions given reports of loss of life in mud slides and the like in northern Italy in the previous two days.

I set off and thought I'd take a route that would see me heading back towards Italy rather than into the Julien Alps.

I decided to pull up after having gone about 10 miles or so and stopped alongside the Soca River. I decided the earlier decision I'd made about my route was wrong.

I reasoned (to myself) that if the weather and road conditions were bad I could mitigate for that by taking more care, stopping, turning back or finding somewhere else to stay en route – but what I couldn't do was mitigate the disappointment I would inevitably have if I didn't stick to my original plan. I would forever ask myself a series of 'what if' questions.

So, that was it – decision made.

I turned around and headed back as per my original plan, which was to head for Srpenica on the banks of the Soca River in Bovec and then onto Zaga, Uccea and then eventually towards Villa Santina, Bolzanno and Trento then down towards Rovereto and then almost back on myself to the Hotel Cime D'oro in Madonna di Campiglio.

It turned out to be the right decision because I went on to have what I can only describe as the most utterly fabulous days riding.

Probably within 15 to 20 minutes of making my decision to turn back, the roads were dry or drying, the scenery superb and there was enough hint of blue sky to confirm to me that the decision to turn back and head this way was the right one.

I knew next to nothing about Slovenia before I travelled there and to be honest I still don't know a great deal, but it really does have a fascinating history and even the most routine of internet research and reading provides a useful and fascinating background and overview of the country's history and move to independence in the late 1980's.

My limited knowledge meant that I wasn't at all sure what to expect – but what I can say, albeit from my short amount of time and travel there is that I found it to be a stunningly beautiful and welcoming country, and one that I would love to go back to at some point.

The mountains, lakes, rivers and roads that I saw as I made my way, provided exceptional sights.

I travelled on into the Dolomites for more of the same and eventually into the Trentino area.

It's really quite difficult to describe how fantastic everything looked, if much of my travels to date had been like seeing the world through High Definition eyes then this was now like having my eyes upgraded to 4K Ultra High Definition – it was glorious beyond description.

I had a good map with me and one that I'd received from an organization called Trentino in Moto which is essentially an association of accommodations hotels etc. that provide good parking for bikes and good local information that is pertinent to bikers.

If you haven't heard of them and you're thinking of biking in the Trento region it's well worth checking out their web site.

It was from studying the low-level map that I decided to head towards Rovereto, a city located in the Vallagarina valley.

Whilst heading in that direction I saw a sign for a pass, the name of which I just can't recall, and that involved taking the SP25 then the SP85 and then eventually the smaller SP53.

I knew that I'd be adding a good amount of time to my day but to head for the pass was a simple decision to make, as I couldn't say with any certainty whether I'd get the opportunity again.

It turned out to be more than worth the effort even though it did mean that I arrived at my hotel in the dark and on damp roads.

By any biking standards today had been a big day and I was tired, ready for a shower and something to eat. I really had enjoyed a great day – so much so that I think it may well have been the best and most complete day I'd ever had on a bike.

The Hotel Cime D'oro is a chalet style hotel about a 10-minute walk from the town centre.

It was pretty quiet but no doubt would be rammed in the skiing season. Check in was straightforward and I was offered the use of the underground garage for my bike.

My room was fairly small but comfortable and the service in the bar was first class.

After a giant sandwich and a couple of beers I was in bed and probably asleep in the time it took for the room to go dark after I'd flicked the switch to off on my bedside light!

Cooler weather

I slept well and woke ready for breakfast and although it was only Thursday morning I definitely had a feeling that this year's trip was drawing to a close.

The weather was cooler (as expected) and my plan was to head into Germany for an overnight stop, then onto Luxembourg on Friday and then finally to Rotterdam on Saturday for the P&O evening sailing and overnight crossing to Hull, in the East Riding of Yorkshire.

Breakfast at the Cime D'Oro was ample and plentiful enough to set me up for the mornings riding. By this stage of the trip my packing routine was more than perfected and it took next to no time at all to pack up neatly and get ready to leave.

After bringing my bike up from the underground garage I clipped the panniers on, went back into the hotel to check out and then headed for the Stelvio Pass.

The Stelvio was around 75 miles or so from my hotel, but it wouldn't exactly be quick to get there given the nature of the roads and in any case I knew that I could take in more than one other pass on the way there.

I headed first for Dimaro about 40 miles northwest of Trento and then onto the nearby small town of Ossana. After that it was Ponte di Legno, Valfurva and Bormio.

Although the town of Bormio is noted for its hot springs a thermal bath wasn't on my agenda that morning.

On my way to Bormio I rode the Passo Campo Carlo Magno, the Passo del Tonale and the Gavia Pass.

The Gavia is a pretty high mountain pass in Lombardy and actually divides the provinces of Sondrio in the north and Brescia in the south.

The scenery was visually stunning, but the pass itself wasn't great.

The Gavia Pass was one of those that although I'm sort of glad I've been on it I would be in no rush to do it again. In many parts the Gavia is narrow, poorly surfaced and in its early stages it's pretty tight.

What it does provide though is stunning views. On the day, I travelled on it the wind was very very strong, so much so that at times it caused me a little concern and at times a feeling of not wanting to be there – it really was that horrible.

There was also another pass before the Tonale that I turned onto and rode but I can't remember its name.

The Campo Carlo and the Tonale were enjoyable and pretty open and flowing.

Eventually I arrived towards the Stelvio Pass, a road that's been on my list to do for a good number of years.

As I made my way onto the Stelvio the wind was blowing an absolute gale – and it made staying upright at times a genuine struggle which took away some of the enjoyment.

I suppose the Stelvio is a pretty iconic pass for many bikers and it's maybe one of the most photographed passes there is.

It is unquestionably beautiful and unquestionably dramatic, at its peak it rises to about 2,750m (over 9,000') and has 48 numbered hairpins up the mountain side.

It is actually the highest paved mountain pass in the eastern alps.

A few years ago it was voted as one of the best driving roads in the world and so it's not at all difficult to see why it is on the 'to do' list of many bikers.

But to be perfectly honest I was left feeling that actually it's a bit overrated and it doesn't make my list of top roads to ride.

Without doubt it is an incredible feat of road engineering and it is amazing in so many ways, but for me the nature of the (mostly) short stretches between hairpins sort of made the effort outweigh the enjoyment, with little opportunity to get into a clear flowing run.

Fortunately, when I was there it was very quiet – and if I was anywhere near the Stelvio in the peak season I'd be sure to give it a miss, I can barely begin to imagine what a chore it might be when rammed with tour buses and tourists.

I'm sure there will be plenty who disagree with me but I genuinely felt it hadn't quite met my expectations – it certainly provides some of the most staggering vistas of winding switchbacks along with exquisite mountain views, but the truth is I wouldn't bother to do it again.

I actually think the Gotthard Pass and some of the nearby passes to it in Switzerland provide more enjoyment (Grimsell, Furka Susten for example) and I'd rather ride the Grossglockner in Austria any day of the week.

But opinions aside – I stopped at the top, took a few pictures and then continued on my way dropping down through a multitude of tight hairpins and generally enjoying the excellent views.

Despite feeling it to be an overrated pass I'd still say it's a 'must do' for a biker.

After coming off the Stelvio I continued on towards Fideris, Vaduz and in the general direction of Konstanz in Germany.

The weather had been mostly decent for the day and although cold and way way too windy on the Stelvio the temperatures had reached a nice 27C in the afternoon as I made my way into Austria.

Off to Germany

In Austria, I rode on yet another pass whose name I just can't recall, but it was one that had wide-open roads complete with sweeping bends and all in all made for some pretty relaxed and easy riding.

I had rain for the latter part of my time in Austria but eventually arrived at my overnight stay in Tengen in Germany.

I'd booked a room at the family run Landgasthof Schutzen hotel and the owner was out to meet me as I pulled up. He's a biker himself and opened his garage for me to leave my bike next to his car for the night.

The owner and his wife were really very welcoming and my room was clean, comfortable and nicely furnished.

It seems a decent location to base yourself for a biking holiday, as it is close to Switzerland, Austria and the Black Forrest – the food is good, the bar has a decent selection of beers and along with the welcoming host it was another overnight stay where all the boxes were easily ticked.

The hotel owner and I chatted about bikes, football (he's a Hamburg fan) and my journey and I'd be pretty happy to recommend this place for a few days if ever you are down that way.

I also chatted with another guest who was staying in the room next to mine, he'd asked me about my bike as he'd seen it as he was checking in at more or less the same time I arrived.

He was having a few days break (driving) but he was a biker and owned a Kawasaki 1200. We spent some time showing each other bike pictures on our phones. He was a nice enough man and I saw him again briefly over breakfast the following morning.

Breakfast was good and plentiful, and not for the first time on this trip I was packed promptly and made an early start and was on the road not long after 08.00am, this time towards the Black Forrest as I decided to do some of the B500 towards Baden Baden, the spa town in Baden-Wurttemberg in southwestern Germany.

I've done the B500 a few times now on various bikes and a couple of times in the car and it's a decent enough road – way way too busy in the peak holiday season and especially at weekends but as I was heading that way on a Friday morning in late September traffic wasn't something that I had to be troubled with.

The first few hours were lovely heading towards Blumberg, Loffingen, Tittisee and Frieberg but the weather was definitely turning cooler and I stopped to swap gloves from the 'shorties' that I'd been wearing for the last couple of weeks to a longer more regular pair of riding gloves.

I'd sort of been meandering my way up towards Luxembourg and had booked myself into a hotel in a place called Kautenbach.

I hadn't really bothered looking at a route as I was pretty familiar with this part of Germany and other than heading for the B500 I just let the day unfold – until I realized at around 13.30 that my almost aimless meanderings had left me a little under 200 miles to the place I'd booked.

The weather looked to be getting darker and I decided to switch to an AutoRoute type road for a while and then was hit by an incredible cloudburst that made road conditions unpleasant.

Not for the first time the change in weather was dramatic and more evidence of the oddly unsettled weather over much of Europe.

The level of spray that was being thrown up from the road surface was almost blinding and I decided that the prudent thing to do was to pull up under a bridge and sit it out.

After 10 or 15 minutes I set off again, back under blue skies and pulled into the next service station for fuel and a bite to eat.

After grabbing a sandwich and a drink I ended up sitting on the kerbside talking to another British biker who it turned out was also heading in the direction of Luxembourg and who had also been on the Stelvio the previous day.

Roadside chat and a decent bloke

Andy from the Wakefield area of England was a really decent bloke and we chatted and swapped stories for around 40 minutes or so.

He'd been on the Stelvio around 17:00 the previous day and in addition to the gale force winds he had to endure rainfall as well – a pretty uncompromising combination on that road.

In fact, he'd seen a couple of bikes on the floor, clearly their riders had not quite managed the bends.

He didn't have anywhere booked and I mentioned to him that the pretty town of Vianden would probably make a decent stopover.

I was quite familiar with Vianden from previous trips as well as having stayed there for a few days earlier in the year with my wife, and I knew there were a number of hotels and B&Bs there some of which advertised as 'biker friendly'.

Andy had been on the road for a couple of weeks and his trip sounded good.

It seemed like we'd been in some of the same, or nearby locations as he too had been down in Italy.

His plan was to book himself onto the P&O crossing from Rotterdam the following evening – so with that and the likelihood that we would meet up again sometime on Saturday night on the boat - we said farewell and I continued on my way to the Hotel Huberty in Kautenbach, itself only about 15 miles from Vianden and where I would have my final night's accommodation on this trip.

Rudi and his apple pie

It was around 18:00 when I got to the hotel and the owner was at the window and waving me straight into his garage – and before I had even taken my helmet and gloves off he was alongside me introducing himself and giving me a warm welcome as well as asking me about my bike.

He also showed me his fabulous machine a new Cam Am, a fascinating three-wheel roadster.

Next it was into the hotel to be introduced to his wife and a couple of guests who were drinking in the bar – quickly followed by questions about my trip – where I had been and where I was going.

Later after getting cleaned up and over a beer I spent time chatting again with Rudi the hotel owner.

He's a warm and friendly bloke who seems to have had his share of decent cars and he definitely likes his Cam Am's, I got the impression that the one sitting in the garage was his second or third.

Rudi spent time showing me various pictures of bikes and cars on his iPad – and it seems that he and his wife do quite well in attracting bikers and car enthusiasts to their pleasant hotel.

My evening meal was great and was cooked by Rudi himself, and if you do stay there (and I can recommend it) then you simply must have some of Rudi's apple pie.

It was different from apple-pie I had previously had and in fact had quite a taste of ginger in it – when I asked him about this he told me it was made to his own recipe and was a popular choice with the many groups of bikers who made the Hotel Huberty a destination and stop off on their weekend ride outs.

The room I'd been allocated was small and comfortable and had the benefit of a great Wi-Fi signal.

I slept particularly well in an extremely comfortable bed. Breakfast on Saturday morning was good and I couldn't help but think I was sure to come back and stay with Rudi and his wife at the Hotel Huberty again at some future date ... and to have some more of Rudi's apple pie.

My packing routine after breakfast was a little different than on previous days.

This time I needed to pack in a way that I could easily just take one bag out of one of the panniers with a change of clothing and overnight gear for the night sailing from Rotterdam.

After that I was on my way leaving behind me the tiny village of Kautenbach and first heading through Luxembourg towards Wiltz on a short but excellent stretch of road, then it was onto Bohey and into Belgium and the towns of Tenneville, Vissenaken and Brecht and then finally onto Rotterdam.

I had no high expectations for my final day – and by now it felt like the trip was all but done.

Damp leaf strewn roads out of Kautenbach had restricted my early morning enjoyment a little and aside from a couple of stops en route to the Europoort at Rotterdam there isn't a great deal to say about Saturdays ride.

Check in was routine at the port of Rotterdam, the largest port in Europe, and the last 15 miles or so to the port serve to illustrate the sheer scale of the surrounding infrastructure, which is home to a huge petrochemical industry that provides an incredibly pervasive diesel like stench to the air.

Although I would have been happy to continue riding across Europe I was also looking forward to going home.

7 - TIME FOR HOME

After check in I took my place pretty much towards the front of the queue for boarding the ferry and as I stood by my bike reflecting a little on the trip the next bike that rolled up to take its place in the queue for the ferry home looked familiar – it was Andy ... the guy I'd met the previous day en route to Luxembourg.

It turned out that Andy had indeed taken me up on my suggestion of heading towards Vianden for his overnight stay on Friday and then like me had sort of just ambled his way up through Luxembourg and Belgium and onto Rotterdam.

Although the ferry didn't sail until about 19:30 we were on board for around 17:30 and we arranged to meet later in one of the bars.

Andy and I did indeed meet later on and it was good to share the evening, complete with a few beers and a bite to eat, with someone who I got on well with and whose company helped make the time pass quickly.

There is little to say about the overnight ferry home – in all fairness the boat seemed to be in much better shape than when I'd last been on it.

It looked like it'd been subject to a decent and well thought out refit and was an altogether better experience than on previous trips, although I still think P&O could learn and make improvements from the service provided by Brittany Ferries.

I woke refreshed and had a coffee along with a cheese and ham croissant for breakfast – it was hardly a substantial breakfast but it was good enough and just about ticked the adequate box.

On all but one previous occasion when I'd made my way home from Hull after a European bike trip it has <u>always</u> rained – but looking towards the coast as the boat made its way into the Port of Hull it was obvious that I would almost certainly be making my way home in bright sunshine and under blue skies.

Final leg

The 107-mile journey home from the King George Dock at the Port of Hull was straightforward.

Most of the final leg of my trip was on the M62, the trans Pennine motorway that connects Liverpool and Hull via Manchester and Leeds, which is actually part of the Euroroute E20 and E22.

Eventually I joined the M60 for all but the last couple of miles to home, and lazily flicked through the readings from the dash looking at the total trip mileage, the average fuel consumption and so on.

Not that any of it made any difference, it's just something I always find myself doing as I get close to home from wherever my ride has taken me.

The weather had remained dry and sunny, and I'd only stopped briefly for fuel. It was a routine, boring incident free journey.

The bike had performed flawlessly, although as you can imagine it was pretty dirty and showed all the road grime you would expect after the best part of 5,000 miles

Apart from the single small scratch after dropping it on the streets of Pompeii it was fine.

I'd filled my riding boots to overflowing over the last few weeks.

I'd travelled through Spain, France, Italy, Austria, Germany, Luxembourg, Belgium and Holland, seen wonderful sights and met wonderful people.

If Northern Spain, the Pyrenees, Languedoc and the Cote d'Azur had been the appetiser then the stunning experience of Italy was the main course.

Riding in the Apennines had been all and more than I expected, my all too brief visits to Pisa, Florence and Sienna tantalised and left me wanting more.

The memory of the walled city of Orvieto will stay with me forever as will the space and light of Tuscany and Umbria.

Where do I begin to really explain how good the icing on the cake was and how happy and exhilarated I felt in Campania as I realised my dream of biking the Sorrento – Amalfi coast road.

And if all of that wasn't enough then Perugia, the capital city of Umbria overloaded me with its magnificence, before the ride across the Venetian flatlands sent my mind and body to sleep – only to be woken again by the beauty of Slovenia.

Trentino was a new and surprising revelation and I must return there one day.

Without doubt I had enjoyed a fabulous journey, pretty much been where I wanted to go and pretty much seen what I wanted to see and plenty more besides.

As the last of my 5,000 miles clicked away I must admit I had begun to think about the next trip.

By around 11.00 on Sunday morning, I turned the last corner of my journey and I was home and this year's road trip was done but it felt good to get home and I was happy to be there.

After the simple pleasure of a cold drink and a refreshing shower I had some serious work to do with a terrific looking welcome home present - a magnificent red velvet cake that had been made for me by Pat.

Until the next time, who could possibly ask for more?

A final word

I hope that you've enjoyed reading this and I'd love to hear from you.

You may also want to read my second motorcycle travel book: **Superbike Across Europe**, available in ebook and paperback.

Please feel free to contact me by email:
1894tony@gmail.com

You can also read more about me and what I'm on my Blog, which you can find at:
https://1894tony.wordpress.com/

Thank you

Tony

Printed in Great Britain
by Amazon